A SUPERFICIAL JOURNEY THROUGH TOKYO AND PEKING

A SUPERFICIAL JOURNEY THROUGH TOKYO AND PEKING

PETER QUENNELL

WITH AN INTRODUCTION BY
GEREMIE BARME

HONG KONG   OXFORD   NEW YORK
OXFORD UNIVERSITY PRESS
1986

Oxford University Press

Oxford New York Toronto
Petaling Jaya Singapore Hong Kong Tokyo
Delhi Bombay Calcutta Madras Karachi
Nairobi Dar es Salaam Cape Town
Melbourne Auckland

and associated companies in
Beirut Berlin Ibadan Nicosia

First published by Faber and Faber Limited 1932
First issued, with permission and with the addition of
an Introduction, in Oxford Paperbacks 1986

ISBN 0 19 584099 2

Printed in Hong Kong by Kings Time Printing Press Ltd.
Published by Oxford University Press, Warwick House, Hong Kong

INTRODUCTION

THE author as traveller is a well-known figure in twentieth-century literature; and some of the more prolific contemporary writers, such as Paul Theroux and Jan Morris, have made careers of travelling. It is still a delight to take walking tours of historical cities or picturesque rural spots accompanied by nothing more than an agreeably written account by a sympathetic writer. In the case of travel in China and Japan today, attempts at such lyricism can prove disheartening. It is often the case that the delight evoked by the personal discovery of what others have seen before is offset by the poignant disappointment that results from being reminded at every step of what was seen, smelt and, more importantly, felt by travellers who passed the same way only a few generations ago. Ours is an age of unprecedented nostalgia. The modern traveller is often driven by a longing for the past; not the world of the ancients, but a recently lost world, the appeal of which is all the greater because it is close enough to be somewhat familiar, though as irretrievable as the Athens of Pericles or Augustan Rome. It is a longing born of a sense of displacement and alienation; yet it is also a nostalgia constantly evoked in the recreations of prose and film, a nostalgia for an elusive mood and a bygone age.

INTRODUCTION

To travel with Peter Quennell on his journey through Tokyo and Peking is, for any reader familiar with these two cities, to come under the spell of unsubstantiated nostalgia, a longing for a past imagined. Quennell is by no means a self-indulgent observer sojourning in the Orient for the sake of wallowing in exotica, or to gather impressions for his career as a writer. He is, however, possessed of an eye for detail and a talent for description that give his record of fleeting impressions gained in a little over a year in Japan and China, a vividness, power, and, dare I even say, relevance that will immediately strike the modern reader. Quennell, born in 1905, came from a renowned family. His parents, Marjorie and C.H.B. Quennell, were social historians, and their highly developed powers of observation coupled with a meticulous scholarship resulted in their unique study, *A History of Everyday Things in England*, the first volume of which appeared in 1918 (Peter Quennell revised the fourth edition of this remarkably popular work in the 1950s). He himself was to write about the common heritage of England and America (*The Past We Share*), although he also engaged in writing projects for a general audience such as the *Time* magazine study, *The Colosseum* (1971).

Travel in the 1930s was by its very nature a type of enforced leisure. Ships and trains provided links between Europe and Asia, and the mere process of removing oneself to a foreign environment was often in itself an experience that justified the undertaking. Moving from one country to another in the days before air travel was a lengthy and languorous process, providing ample time for reflection and anticipation. More often, however, the traveller's dream-like visions of his *terra incognita* would fade as the

sodden reality of the destination encroached on his senses.
Quennell mused on the philosophy of travel not long after
his arrival in Japan: '. . . to set out on a journey is to start
the Romantic upon its travels in the opposite direction,
due to pass one in mid-career toward one's goal . . . .' In
an age when Japan still bore a superficial yet distinct
physical resemblance to its feudal past, despite four decades
frantically expended in becoming 'modern', Quennell was
a sober observer, quick to see that '. . . the real country
one goes in search of whether it be the real England or
the real Japan — is everywhere and also nowhere as you
please, far away and immediately underfoot'.

Quennell arrived in Tokyo in 1931, eight years after the
devastating earthquake of 1923 obliterated much of the
Edo of the Shoguns that had survived the progressive
rigours of the Meiji era. As one can see from the contemporary photographs in such works as *The Reconstruction
of Tokyo* (1933), a massive self-congratulatory study of the
rebuilding of the striken city published under imperial
aegis, Tokyo had become, and still remains today, a low-
lying concrete and metal growth over the Kanto plain
highlighted only by chunky blockhouses in the interna-
tional style for banks and government buildings. It is a
sprawling city marked by monotony and confusion,
unrelieved by any hint of grand vision or true squalor.

These were the early years of the Showa reign (now in
its sixtieth year), and Quennell was 26. Evelyn Waugh
was nearly the same age when, some years earlier, he had
done the milk-run around the Mediterranean by ship,
which he described in *Labels*. Waugh's avowed aim was
to get to Russia and perhaps from there to venture as far
as China and Japan. It was fashionable for writers to

experience the Far East: Somerset Maugham (who was a friend of Quennell), Noel Coward, Harold Acton, Osbert Sitwell, and William Empson are but a few of the men of letters who travelled, lived and wrote in Asia, using China as a backdrop for some of their works.

Quennell came to Japan just as the liberalism spawned by the Meiji era and nurtured in the Taisho period was approaching its jerky and bloody end. Premier Hamaguchi, whose resignation in April 1931 marked the failure of Japan's pre-war dalliance with parliamentary democracy, was shot at Tokyo Station in an assassination attempt only months before Quennell's arrival. He makes passing mention of the incident and the Premier's reported recovery before going on to comment on the Imperial Hotel, Frank Lloyd Wright's 'feverish dream' next to Hibiya Park; a building that is sorely missed today, having been replaced by a gleaming and featureless example of functional post-modern architecture some years ago.

Although political events hardly infringe on Quennell's meditations on Japan, the author is nonetheless keenly aware of social realities. He senses a disturbing unbending element in the Japanese character, one that was to come increasingly to the fore in the 1930s and make a mockery of the country's Western-style enlightenment. 'It is as though a shy and egocentric man,' Quennell writes, 'who yearns for the society of his fellow mortals, for the cheerful promiscuity of everyday life, should attempt with periodic and desperate violence to wrench free from his own innate reserve. He is determinedly sociable but always lonely. Sooner or later, the introspective mood returns, his spirit bends back upon itself; and so Japan, after every spasm of change, has retired once more to airless isolation.'

INTRODUCTION

Quennell is prepared to be impressed by Japanese society, as are so many latter-day travellers, and businessmen. But his fourteen months of contact with students who expected him to be a foreign *sensei*, an oracle of Western learning, were a definite imposition on him. The fantasies he had entertained before reaching Japan of teaching his course on English literature to an assembly of Zen monk scholars in the austere surroundings of a tatami hall were shattered the first time he walked into the dusty lecture-hall at his university, the atmosphere of which reeked of the public school. His 'acolytes' were students dressed in uniforms that gave them the appearance of tram-conductors. Although employed to lecture on English literature, after the first class in which his students sat in absolute silence failing to comprehend anything he said, Quennell was reduced to dictating all of his lectures in the manner of Lafcadio Hearn. He found himself trapped in the role of schoolmaster, and felt that his extra-curricular attempts to communicate with Japanese people went similarly unrewarded. The passivity of his students and the meaningless queries of his Japanese colleagues must have grated on a man who was to go on to write studies of Pope, Byron, Ruskin, and Dr Johnson, edit a history magazine and produce a comprehensive history of English literature. In the end, his scepticism about Japan left him with grave doubts about the achievements of the new age, and time and again he sought solace in the traditional theatre. His delicate descriptions of Kabuki, No, and Puppet theatre, along with profiles of famous performers, reveal a highly perceptive understanding of the traditional though somewhat stultified Japanese aesthetic.

INTRODUCTION

Contact with Japanese youth and an insight into native education methods gave Quennell a preview of the inner workings of what is nowadays lauded as the 'Japanese miracle'. He wrote, 'You cannot pour into the minds of worker-ants a highly individualist philosophy and hope that they will remain unperturbed.' Although worded in a way that would perhaps only appeal to Common Market analysts of the Japanese economy, his concern touched on the schizophrenic nature of the country that today more than ever results in complex tensions and unassuaged frustrations throughout the society.

But it was the palpably oppressive atmosphere of Japan more than anything else that fuelled Quennell's disenchantment. '. . . Japan is as airless and hard to breathe in as an old building filled with whirring modern machinery.' And it was with a sigh of 'overwhelming relief' that he embarked for China from Kobe during his spring vacation.

For Quennell China meant Peking, and the vast tawny plains of the north. The imperial city was progressively stripped of its power and prestige by the change of government in 1911, and the relocation of the capital to Nanking in the late 1920s. In Quennell's day the Peking of foreign travellers was in fact home for displaced hostesses from Surrey and Chelsea, with their naïve attempts to create an atmosphere of the 'real China' in their cluttered courtyard houses, which were often a cross between museums and antique shops, or temple retreats in the Western Hills. The foreign community in the city were obsessive collectors, specializing as the case may be in jade bibelots, bronze ritual vessels, fine porcelain, or simply exotic memories. Harold Acton describes these 'worshippers and exploiters of the past' with considerable verve in *Peonies and Ponies*. Added to this were the Westernized Chinese who were accorded a welcome at many 'At Homes' by the Western sinophiles as living proof of the Chinese cultural renaissance. They fluttered decorously about the damasked edges of this latter-day Legation society nostalgic for their student days in the West, remaining both fascinated and repulsed by their hosts. Then there were the remnants of court nobility and the hangers-on, old Manchu princelings and their families, petty gangsters and profiteers. Even the intellectual ferment that had enlivened the universities in the 1920s had died out; meanwhile the endless wars and economic deprivations that ravaged the country continued to take their toll on the city and the lifestyle of its inhabitants.

But Quennell was not interested in searching out some local colour for a novel or a play, nor had he travelled to Peking to become one of the temporary acquisitions of some avaricious hostess. He went there as much to flee one environment as to find another. His travels in the north, from the port at Taku to Tientsin and then on to Peking, were short and his contact with the country fleeting at best. But he found China as different from Japan as he could have wished. The tame beauty of Honshu seemed all the more claustrophobic when compared with the arid and tomb-ridden vistas of North China. As he wrote later in an essay entitled 'Chinese Poetry', 'The Chinese landscape seems an enormous vacuum, and you, the traveller, poised on its edge, solitary and insignificant as, except in instants of deep physical and nervous dejection, you have never felt before.'*

---

* See Peter Quennell, *The Singular Preference: Portraits and Essays* (London, 1952).

INTRODUCTION

The Peking that Quennell visited was the city describ-ed in loving detail by writers such as Juliet Bredon and Lin Yutang. Both the city and the style of life it afforded its citizens are gone forever, energetically wiped out by the revolutionary wilfulness of Mao Tse-tung and his town-planners. Some of the more famous landmarks do, however, remain. We can still explore the Imperial Palace with Quennell and proceed to Peihai Park with its massive white dagoba. The author's descriptive talent lies not in inspiring digressions on Peking's walls or pleasances, but rather in his delicate limning of such seemingly trivial tnings as the grotesquely shaped goldfish in tubs, the 'Bourbons or the Hapsburgs of their breed', which are still to be found in Peihai Park. Fresh from Japan where the simple lines and natural colours of the Sung dynasty lived on in temple and residential architecture, the Ch'ing taste accepted as 'Chinese' struck him as heavy and un-palatable, and he ponders the question of when 'this pas-sion for the grotesque, for shapes bulbous, writhen and twisted, gnarled and bent, first made its appearance in the Chinese world. . . .' Ironically, it is just this aspect of Chinese art, a decadent and mongrel aesthetic rigidly ap-plied by the Manchus to all public and religious buildings — that 'gimcrack of Chinese fantasy', a *petit bourgeois* love of bric-à-brac — that has come to represent the most visi-ble legacy of the country's past, and we now see it endlessly reproduced not only in new hotels in China but even in restaurants and gardens and private homes overseas. As Quennell commented in his essay on Chinese poetry, 'A host of Western scholars and explorers have helped to clarify our understanding of the Chinese background, and have demonstrated, for example, that what was once considered the flower of Chinese art and craftsmanship — the scroll-paintings, jades and lacquers of the age of Ch'ien Lung — was, in fact, the debased offshoot of a declining civilization.'

Nonetheless, there is something special in the atmosphere of Peking, an elusive quality that, despite the ravages of thirty years of proletarianization, can still be found today; it is something that a traveller from Tokyo or any other modern metropolis can savour with pleasure — '. . . under the even flow of Japanese life one reaches down to a fundamental lack of sympathy, and in China, for all its desolation, are still traces of a world one can comprehend'.

Yet Quennell's perceptions of China, like those of Japan, are far from being limited to mannered comments on local sights and observations on art. His asides on the political confusion of China in the 1930s — years when war-lords tussled with the invading Japanese and the Nationalist government in Nanking — are penetrating and at times highly illuminating even for the modern reader. Peking was then, as it is now, a city of political gossip. And the rumours always centred around the intrigues of a small number of families, their alliances, manoeuvres, and stratagems. 'Parochial — perhaps that is the right word', Quennell comments after relating the latest doings of the Young Marshal, Chang Hsien-liang. 'I had already noticed how China at its most horrific has a homeliness which is reflected by the foreign papers; and, in the gossip which sometimes came our way, there was always the same note of quiet provincialism. Any attempt to find a clue through Chinese politics seemed to lead direct into a small and airless room, crowded with the members of a single family.' In these few words Quennell, a casual observer of Chinese life, a traveller on a superficial journey during a term-break, sums up realities of Chinese politics and life in a way that so often eludes the clever analyses of the professional China-watcher. 'It is just a big problem of family life, the politics of an overcrowded tenement, if you imagine a tenement as co-existing with, or being raised on the foundations of, a huge necropolis.'

The spectre of the dead, and of the past, still holds sway in China. 'Reformers, who were revolutionary during their lifetime, become aristocrats in the hierarchy of the dead.' Sun Yat-sen was to replace Confucius, and it is now the spirit of another reformer-turned-ruler that haunts the country. 'The past assimilates the present: Chronos perpetually devours his children: Athena springs from the head of Jove, only to sink back again' ('Chinese Poetry').

GEREMIE BARMÉ

A SUPERFICIAL JOURNEY
THROUGH
TOKYO AND PEKING

SANDANJI ICHIKAWA IN 'KANJINCHO' AS THE
SHOGUN'S OFFICER

A

SUPERFICIAL JOURNEY

THROUGH

TOKYO AND PEKING

BY

PETER
QUENNELL

LONDON
FABER AND FABER LIMITED
24 RUSSELL SQUARE

TO
N.Q.

AUTHOR'S NOTE

Most travel books written at the present day seem to fall into one of two categories; there is the book which consists of an ordinary time-table, embellished with thumb-nail sketches on the margin to show the author in his adventures and misadventures, enjoying a good meal or catching a train; and there is the guide book, the illuminated Baedeker, digressive, sentimental or romantic. . . .

Neither method was quite suited to my needs, and this book, if I may be allowed to prompt my critic, should be regarded as a kind of travel film, a sequence in which image suggests image. Emphatically, it is not a book 'about' Japan; I spent a year there but cannot pretend to 'know the country'. Let me admit that my point of view is superficial and trust to the fascination of the subject.

My debts of gratitude are numerous and deep; but, since it is possible that certain of my creditors might prefer not to be mentioned on this page, I will confine myself to thanking my friend, Mr. John Hayward, for the great kindness he has shown in reading through the typescript, and the Editor of the *New Statesman & Nation* for permission to make use of two articles which have been rewritten and incorporated in the text.

CONTENTS

CONTENTS

ILLUSTRATIONS

ILLUSTRATIONS

PART I

TOKYO

CHAPTER I

AN EARTHQUAKE

Earthquakes are often preceded by a deep stillness and are followed by a short interval of the same hush. It was very dark, with the dense obscurity of the early morning, and we had been awakened in our cramped bedroom beneath the tiles by an odd violent movement of roof and floor, a creaking and straining, the lurch forward of our entire universe, as though its solid scheme were preparing to fly apart, all accentuated by a fierce rattling of loose panes. Forwards and backwards, forwards and backwards, a sickly plunge, like the plunging course of a small ship in a heavy sea. And it was in no steamer that we were weathering out the storm, but in the high wooden carcass of an old hotel.

It came to rights; the universe reinstated itself; and meanwhile there had been nothing to do but lie and listen. Screens and windows, the rafters and the floor-boards, had proved vocal, each complaining in a different tongue, loudly shuddering, sharply tacking or painfully wheezing, as the building leant forward on its motionless journey. ... On and on; it may have lasted a matter of seconds. It seemed interminable but quite suddenly came to an end.

15

The tempest passed, and you could hear it passing away, in a vibration which dwindled audibly along the silence; softer and softer, the rumbling retreat of a heavy vehicle which through the London night rushes ominously beneath your window and dwindles back again into the nowhere from which it has sprung.

A brief silence; but like a tree-load of awakened starlings the other inmates of the hotel began to move. Lights were turned on and, as I looked into the corridor, a young man in a cotton kimono, with rumpled hair, stepped out under the blazing electric globe, peered around him and stepped back, shutting his door. Below our casement on the slope of the zinc roof, a woman who was squatting there like a draggled pigeon, the thick meshes of her black coiffure all awry, talked noisily to some invisible friends above. The telegraph wires were still vibrating; but they too reassumed their habitual droop. The draggled woman crept in and closed her window. Silence again, and a sense of approaching dawn.

Then *Oooomm!* went the bell of a near-by shrine, the sound expanding like a dark bubble in the pellucid quiet —*Oooomm!*—more like a drum than like a bell, as a beam thudded deliberately against the bronze and the metallic bubble expanded and grew thinner. A disturbing sound; I very often woke to hear it and never escaped the pang of strangeness which it brought home—or a watchman who perambulated the narrow lanes and clapped together two pieces of smooth wood. I saw him afterwards, his straw hat and his paper lantern, and heard him, when a fire had broken out, announcing stridently the neighbourhood and the address; very odd through the dead interval before the dawn that hoarse voice which cried in a foreign language, and the clap-clapping which marked his foot-steps down the street.

We had been living in Japan now nearly a month, and had long ago forgotten our reason for coming. Perhaps it was to hear the bell of a Buddhist temple, in some shabby backwater behind a street with shops and trams, announcing a further day and fresh perplexities. Rather romantic; a new *frisson*, one must admit, to hear the shivering notes of the thudded bell spread lugubrious over tumbled acres of grey roofs, just emerging as the darkness slowly thinned. . . . Alas, that to set out on any journey is to start the Romantic upon its travels in the opposite direction, due to pass one in mid-career toward one's goal. It travels fast, and was now inhabiting London where it loitered about the street where we had lived. I remembered the disc of water in a London park which I had sometimes rounded on cold autumn and winter mornings when little waves hurried slapping against its verge and russet water-birds swam up through the light mist which clung in wisps and strays to its steely surface—that or overheated London evenings when a violet fog had collected around the lamps and the polished pavements hummed to a passing wheel. . . .

But then the Romantic—we have at any rate this consolation—is quick to fill the void which we leave behind. It wells up, like marsh water into hollow footprints, and we see our tracks as a succession of silver pools. Thus I can picture now, with a clarity which is almost tender, the hotel in which our first month was spent. It stood at some distance from the main road, amid a labyrinth of grey roofs and shabby fences, its steep red facade and pretentious tower emerging haughtily from the shadows of a small cul-de-sac. I did not notice, when for the first time I crossed its threshold, that the frontage, which wore the appearance of brick and stone, was an insubstantial mask of hammered tin nailed carefully over a foundation of lath and plaster; in fact, that the hotel was all face. . . . But 'face' and its importance in my new life was a phenomenon I had not begun to understand. We entered and the proprietor of the hotel was summoned by a maidservant from a back room.

When he appeared it was with the broad and burnished smile which afterwards very seldom left his features. He was young, largely built for a Japanese; he was good-natured and his widowed mother in the background hovered, palpably inquisitive and also smiling, as the explanation and bargaining went on. I can still follow him as he led us down the passage and up and down into various unpromising rooms. The 'Western-style' rooms we were shown first, a few meagre chambers in a separate wing, furnished with iron bedsteads, washing-stands and wicker chairs. We declined them, for the ball-fringe of the green tablecloth, a china ash-tray, the basin and the jug made up a still-life which was too significant and too painful. Then we asked to see the Japanese part of the building where we settled ourselves, deciding to sleep upon the floor.

Two rooms, a bedroom and a larger sitting-room, now became the constricted orbit in which we moved. They were at the top and to the rear of the tall edifice, and the sitting-room had an extensive view of suburban hillside and, far away, of—'Fuji!' said the proprietor proudly, pointing with a vague gesture over the roofs to a factory chimney smoking against the horizon. Much later, as if completing the advertisement and paying a graceful tribute to the hotel which bore its name, Mount Fuji drew the curtains which hid its snow-cap and took its call in a dim zone of misty azure. Always a little impeded by the smoking chimney, it struggled forth as a pale nick on the furthest skyline. For an hour or two it glimmered unreal and distant, so remote that it seemed never to have touched the ground; then it vanished and the slender spire of the modern cathedral wafted its thin plume without challenge across the sky.

CHAPTER II

THE HOTEL

That was enough; face was saved, which was all-important. The hotel had lived up to its sounding name. We too, I imagine, in a minor way were contributing to the 'face' of the young proprietor by our continued if incongruous presence beneath his roof. Foreigners are more trouble than Japanese. They are like sea-fish in a small fresh-water aquarium, twisting and noisily blundering around its walls till the translucency has become turbid with sheer annoyance. And they are helpless; the live coals in the charcoal brazier are forgotten by them and perpetually go out. They have odd habits; they drink the viscous juice of cows. They eat heavily and cannot sit upon the floor.

A trifle suspect both in manners and personal customs, they have a face-value in this modern progressive world. They are imported to teach at the large universities—which accounted for the presence at the hotel of the young foreigners who lived secluded in an upper room where they sometimes wore their slippers upon the mats. . . . Those mats! Every respectable Japanese sloughs his shoes at the doorstep when he comes in, exchanging them for a pair of felt or leather slippers. His slippers he again drops when he enters a room, when he goes to the bath or visits the privy or the urinal. Else a sticky polish from the boards may be trodden into the fine weave of the clean *tatami*, which are expensive and the pride of a decent house. And maybe there is something symbolically right and proper in the shuffling halt before one crosses the inner door-sill.

We ourselves, when we settled down in our matted room, were playing a game with rules which we did not know. From the Japanese standpoint it was a biggish room, measured, as rooms are measured, in terms of mats —and very rightly, for they were its charm and its chief equipment, beautiful *tatami* of a subdued golden lustre, put down in long rectangles edged with braid which split up with pleasant precision the glistening floor.

There were the mats, then, a low knee-table of polished wood, a few cushions, the porcelain brazier and a lacquered clothes horse; otherwise little or nothing except a picture which hung in a small alcove upon the right. Little and yet sufficient for a Japanese, who would have made tea from the iron kettle upon the brazier and absorbed cupfuls of the insipid pale-green brew, drinking them off in three gulps as custom requires. . . . We realized on how substantial a margin of comfort our life till the present day had always depended, for discomfort, as one understands it in Western countries, would have been comfort or perhaps luxury in our new surroundings. And afterwards I came to divine in Western literature the significance of the environment that gave it birth—the tremendous background of couches and downy beds, thick carpets and easy chairs and shuttered windows.

For us even the traditional native luxury was difficult to come by and hard to keep. Getting a bath was a business of some skill and a test of courage once the bath had been secured. It was seldom heated before the late afternoon, since the Japanese do not bathe in the early morning. You passed the kitchen on slipper-sloppering soles, undressed in a tiny matted ante-room and descended into the steamy depths of a cemented cell. Washing must be done outside the bath, and for this purpose there was a row of brass-bound tubs, a wooden stool and several fragments of hard loofah. The Western bath is a typically Western institution, a habit perfected by the individualism of the nineteenth century. Every man may dispose of his own bath and can wash, read or sleep in it just as he likes. When he has finished he allows it prodigally to run away, a soapy libation to the dark gods of the sewer-world. . . .

This is illogical; it is anti-social into the bargain, and the Japanese, after washing upon the floor, dips himself into the water of a scalding tank which he enjoys in common with a long series of unknown bathers. Looked at sensibly, there is no reason why the same bath should not serve for the refreshment of all alike; and yet in practice it is often with a certain repugnance that one lowers oneself towards the oozy bottom of a strange cistern and sees its cloudy wavelets mounting towards one's chin.

The water itself was usually quite clean, but this semi-virginity was more repulsive than genuine dirtiness. It felt used-up and was apt to affect the nerves as a too-experienced innocence affects the emotions. So that when an opaque fragment came to the surface—which happened disconcertingly from time to time, no doubt through some imperfection of the ancient pipes—one was not disposed to give it the benefit of a decent doubt and rose and crawled forth on to the swimming floor.

At this moment, there was often a precipitate entry by another visitor in a cotton bath-robe with a printed towel. He would look surprised and withdraw at a mumbled protest; the mysterious occident must be permitted to have its foibles, not the least of them being a selfish regard for privacy and the perverted charm which its poets and painters have found in nakedness. . . . Meanwhile, red and flustered after his bath, the enigmatic occidental would leave the bathroom, skirting the hotel kitchen as before. The kitchen, which was open on three sides, contained five or six servants hard at work, who watched the passer-by with inquisitive vague faces. Equally inquisitive was the calm scrutiny of the proprietor's mother, a stout woman; the days were growing hot and her kimono might be rolled down as far as the waist, showing a flaccid frog-like torso and drooping dugs.

Back again to the cantankerous privacy of the upper room, leaving behind the kitchen-odour and the smell of sewage, particularly strong at the foot of the steep stairs, to the familiar scent of mats and smouldering charcoal which pervaded, not unpleasantly, the stranger's fortress. This stronghold, at most times undisturbed, had been on one occasion the object of a short siege. Periodically the quiet hotel was occupied by youths and girls from a middle-school in some remote province, brought up to admire the sights of the modern capital. Then the building hummed and seethed, and the smallest rooms brimmed over with a dozen noisy occupants whose clamours sounded almost until midnight. Bedchambers were then

so packed with chirruping girls that each cubby-hole gave
forth the noise of an excited aviary or of a hundred mar-
mosets twittering in unison. On other days, they were
young men who filled the corridors, and it was among
these that the story got about of two eccentric foreigners
living on the top floor.

Every middle-school boy has learned some English,
but there are few who have met and spoken with a living
foreigner. How natural that, in the proximity of two
specimens, male and female, both reputed exceedingly
odd, an attempt should be made to interview the exotic
creatures after they have retired to a couple of pallets in
their temporary cage! . . . This attempt, from the point of
view of the cornered animals, was first manifested by a
stealthy gathering of stockinged feet, a sibilant rumour
interrupted by staccato giggles, and the stir of a crowd
where none is anxious for the first place. It drew nearer,
becoming solid beyond the door. There was a pause.
What did they expect to find within? What questions of
natural history and Western ethics would they propound
once their quarry was in view?

Judging at any rate by the stupefaction of the serried
hunters, they had not expected that the animal would
turn, bursting out at them as they stood clustered before
his lair and haranguing them in a wild flood of foreign
speech. On both sides the experience was worth having.
There is a moment in the mental processes of a Japanese
when a shock has not had time to lead to action and a
complete blankness paralyses every faculty. The unexpected will always find him at a loss, and the unexpected
apparition from the upper room, outlandish and absurd in
his flapping dressing-gown, seemed to act like a fire-hose

upon the crowd who trooped away docile and speechless towards their rooms.

One's nerves are seldom good in a foreign climate, and the whole episode, though ludicrous, had been unsettling. Early manhood is a horrid period of human life, for the body and the mind resemble dough, unleavened and un-baked in its lumpish pallor. . . . About Japanese youths there is something especially doughy, and the sight of the crowded faces beyond the door, some shock-headed, some spectacled and close-cropped, made me reflect that as a pedagogue I should never succeed, if only through lack of sympathy with my raw material. Pedagogy, like siphilis, is in the blood; but thank heavens that its dis-semination is less widespread. Yes, the prospect was cer-tainly a little dark and no more beckoning than the tum-bled suburban landscape, which could be studied if one pushed back the sliding shutters—verdant tree-tops, grey roofs and smoking chimneys, set to music by the faint screech of a passing tram.

But there were consolations; below us in the shadowy courtyard some crooked boughs had begun to blossom with scarlet buds and, if curious faces in the opposite windows peered and goggled, we too had our revealing glimpses of an alien world. Not far off stood a chocolate-painted girls' school, of which the boarders lived in a lodging-house across the alley. We could command with-out interruption from our bedroom casement the narrow room in which they slept and did their work, innocent dumpy girls of seventeen whom it was a great pleasure to watch embroidering or painting flowers, or plucking a queer instrument with many strings, like a gigantic zither laid upon the mats. At dawn the thin pallets on which they lay were rolled up and out of sight into a cupboard, and from that time only their industrious squatting shapes furnished and decorated the bleak chamber that was their home.

English hymn-tunes sometimes beguiled their diligent hours, high and nasal—the mere ghost of a strangled melody—often repeated till one had guessed their probable origin. Flightier and more ambiguous was the sound of voices which reached us now and then in our own hotel, from a room beneath ours on the next floor, where the bedraggled lady, who during the recent earthquake had taken refuge on the flat roof outside her window, lived alone and tired her hair and whitened her neck at a tall glass in front of a single cushion. Her dressing-table, which one caught a glimpse of when the door was open, exemplified the sober qualities of true elegance, some long hairpins, little boxes in lacquer trays, a wooden comb, printed face-cloths hung to air and a large pot of the universal *o shiroi*—which rendered literally means 'honourable wet-white'.

The tall mirror itself was always shrouded, for mirrors among old-fashioned Japanese are treated with a certain superstitious delicacy which implies a connection between the image and the human soul. . . . We liked that; it gave a touch of the 'genuine thing' to an existence at once perplexing and unmysterious, at the same moment enigmatic and highly banal. Here at all events was a reminder, however weak, of the young women whom Utamaro drew at their toilet, painting their lips with a tiny brush or fixing their coiffure with sharp cruel-looking pins. 'The real Japan?' one hazarded, passing by; a foolish remark, since the real country one goes in search of—whether it be the real England or the real Japan—is everywhere and also nowhere as you please, far away and immediately underfoot. Thus it is possible that a Japanese living in Bayswater might learn as much of England during his stay as if he explored systematically the entire realm—as much and conversely just as little as there was room for in his particular mental scheme.

At this moment Japan—*our* Japan—consisted principally of the hotel and the hotel-life, eked out by long pilgrimages across the city on various errands which we were seldom able to perform. Destinations proved uncommonly elusive; Tokyo has no street-names and no house-numbers, but the ward—or the *ku*—contains the *chome*, which again is subdivided into the *cho*, which includes a wide range of numbered departments, which may designate not one but several houses. . . . Even a being more intelligent than the average taxi-driver might lose his road in such a dædal of tangled addresses, and a Japanese will not admit that he has lost his bearings till he is buried deep in the muddy labyrinth of a strange quarter.

Then he pulls up and looks round for your assistance. You are in a narrow street bordered by grey fences, by hooded gates, by concrete gutters on either side which make it impracticable for the car to turn its wheels; a little lighted shop in the far distance, an electric lamp shining on ragged evergreens; the knowledge that you are already twenty minutes late and a stolid face impassively regarding you. . . . Added together, the total sum of such hopeless wanderings would amount to whole days or entire weeks. They produced upon a newcomer's imagination the effect of inhabiting continuously a dream-world, in which one reached one's goal by walking the wrong way.

Very often our host, if we were going to dine, would come out himself to aid the search and spring up suddenly at the mouth of a murky passage, holding an umbrella as he peered stoically down the lane.

We disembarked; hospitality, congratulations, in a little house, half foreign and half Japanese, tightly wedged among other little houses which gathered round with an odd air of secretive intimacy. For the time being it was Old England or Old Oxford. But not for long—the reminiscences and the random small-talk were as diaphanous as the smoke of the cigarettes, and the neighbourhood, with a smell or a burst of noise, flooded in through the wide-open paper windows. Foreigners scratch the surface of Japanese life, and exist, as it were temporarily, in their own dwellings. The casual makeshift atmosphere of the huge metropolis is too pervasive to be withstood for a length of years, and very soon the best-established foreign stronghold takes on the impermanent flimsy look of its immediate neighbours.

Flimsy—the word belongs to Japanese life, flimsy buildings in flimsy tattered vegetation, a flimsy landscape where the mountains have no roots, but stand up two-dimensional out of the mist, for all the world as though they were clipped from coloured foil. In terms of flimsiness, it would have been difficult to go further than life as we were leading it on the top floor, trunks still packed and the few belongings which came to hand looking awkward and self-conscious in their strange environment. We ate flimsily, and on the way to our vague luncheons sometimes paused to watch the houses which were being built at the end of the lane leading to the hotel. Sooner or later we ourselves should need a house, and we marked their growth with the beginnings of personal interest.

They were thrown up, particularly the house at the street-corner, almost as rapidly as the booths at a country fair, a thin skeleton of white wood freshly sawn taking to itself first a coat of wattle-and-daub, then hurrying on clapboards and a tile roof; after which it was practically ready for occupation. June closed and in the last week of the rainy month we agreed to become the tenants of the corner house and moved away with all our belongings down the lane. The proprietor, who, as the hot season grew more oppressive, often appeared, solid and virile, in a suit of undergarments, seemed genuinely a little reluctant to let us go. Otherwise our departure made no stir; though the crippled watchdog still barked at us if we happened to meet.

CHAPTER III

A HOUSE IN THE RAIN

U nlike all other Japanese institutions, the Rainy Season—by Japanese it is called the Nyubai— pays no heed to the scheduled course marked out for it, but will drag on by determined fits and starts sometimes into the middle of summer months. It had been raining during the better part of June, and it was raining as we moved and settled in. The cloudy sky deepened to a dark indigo and the rain fell heavily and continuously, rattling through the pointed dusty leaves of the lank bushes which grew up against the house. Rain here was not accompanied by freshness, but seemed to heighten instead of lowering the temperature. It shut in the occupants of the wooden house behind a palisade of glimmering vertical lines, which drove steadily down from the dusky air, each line meeting the earth in a little fountain and welling muddily till the whole garden was under water.

The glass and the paper screens would be pushed back; the electric fan would buzz in the lower rooms. Since this cataract seldom shifted from the vertical, one could sit for coolness almost out of doors, the rain descending solidly

past the eaves, the gutters choking and gurgling overhead, as one listened to the screech of a distant tram, to
the sound of clogs in the alley beyond the wall, to the insects still stridulating in the garden and the noise of the
fan which turned slowly from left to right. . . .

Those noises, so insistent and so monotonous—how
vivid in their suggestion of that time! Always, at every
season of the year, from the narrow lane which ran beside
the house, came a perpetual slipper-sloppering of wooden
clogs. After a snowfall, it is true, we scarcely heard them;
but in dry weather they rang out loud and flat, and in the
rain acquired a sonorous squeaking note as they splashed
from puddle to puddle along the road. We heard, too, the
faint twanging of the raindrops as they struck the oiled
surface of an umbrella. The windows only looked out on
to the garden, but, if you pushed open the sliding door
into the street, the coloured translucent discs of passing
umbrellas gave a certain life and charm to the rainy day.
They were very big and the luminous shade they cast
surrounded the face in a peculiar sickly glow, rather becoming if the face they happened to shelter was the pale
moon-shaped countenance of a young woman, with her
skirts tucked up over a scarlet petticoat and a strip of
brownish leg beyond the sock.

On the whole, we preferred to remain indoors; it was
the effect of the climate and of Japan. Indoors and out of
doors were much alike—for a house from which an entire
wall can be taken away never produces an air of great
seclusion; while there was something in the prevalent
warmth and dampness that gave a sense of being perpetually under cover. Even the rain, which glistened steadily
past the windows, suggested the gigantic leakage of a

faulty roof; and, a year later when we visited a Berlin restaurant where a storm sweeps once every half-hour across a pasteboard panorama of moonlit Rhineland, I recognized the comparison for which I had been looking—the same dead glistening streaks of water, the same unearthly, unnaturally diffused light.

Butterflies skimmed to and fro beneath the downpour, large tattered swallowtails, brown or black—big powdery things blundering through the rain, flapping into the dryness of the little house, struggling forth to vanish amid the foliage which shone dully in the dull gleam of a livid sky. There was a cicada on a tree-trunk in the garden which whirred antiphonal to a cicada beyond the fence. We heard it but could never find its hiding-place, till one day—the sky was clear and the sun was hot—it tumbled and lay helpless upon the ground, a fat fallen dryad with gauzy wings, afterwards slaughtered by a predatory kitten among the azaleas.

For two kittens the whole garden at this time was a repository stocked with strident mechanical toys. . . . They would slip off the step and under the rain and return with a struggling cricket between their teeth, letting it drop to jump and twist upon the mats, running it down again with the most delicate of cruel paws. Mangled insects, and whiskery remnants left uneaten, were often deposited and often swept up around the room. It made no odds; the chirruping chorus was still in strength; another cicada did its best on the identical tree, while some frogs, in the more extensive neighbouring plot, quacked and gurgled loudly into the darkness.

Though full of life, our garden was very small; but, though small, it was densely grown with various shrubs.

They banked up in a straggling line along the fence, queer evergreens with five-fingered glossy leaves which throve prodigiously yet always looked dishevelled—a characteristic inherent in their constitution and the strange method of growth they have adopted. These bushes, much cultivated by the Japanese, remain weedy larrikins until they die. Long stems, smooth and pallid as those of the fig, radiate at acute angles from the soil, each supporting a single tuft of leaves and producing branches which conscientiously repeat their action. About May they bring to birth a sticky spire; it wilts like a melting candle and presently falls, soon followed by last year's sallow leaves which have curled back disclosing a new tuft. More unstable with every inch they gain in height, the weak limbs crack hideously beneath the snow or sag and nod despairing to the ground. Hapless and disconsolate on stormy days, they are oppressive and close-smelling in the warm weather, when they assume a pose of stringy self-importance and collect dust in the sprawling shadow around their feet.

Azaleas also flowered in the garden, two dwarf trees with red and white paper trumpets, and a camellia, rather woody and past its prime, somewhat harassed by the ugly imminence of the larger bushes. Several trees from the narrow space left open stood up stiffly like tall travellers in a crowded railway carriage. The middle tree, the tallest, was quite dead, a mere gaunt decapitated ruin which sported a few leaves as dead as itself in a meagre buttonhole half way towards its summit. The Japanese have a fondness for decaying wood, which they extend to stones round or oddly shaped—any stone if it is round enough and large enough. And, being householders of modest

C

but decent condition, our stones were small in bulk but pleasantly smooth, useful as stepping-stones when the weather was very wet and vaguely suggestive of some immemorial cataclysm which had washed them up into the tiny garden upon its course. . . .

There they lay as at the bottom of a deep aquarium, in the dim aquarium light which came from above, their round surface striped and mottled by greenish shadows, reposing in a red spilth of sodden azalea-petals. During the rainy months everything grows fast and the roughest slip, stuck casually into the ground, takes hold and begins to flourish its bright leaves, almost before you have forgotten the naked twig. Everything sprouts; the aspidistras near the fence—plants one does not associate with life and energy—unfurl a fresh green from their dismal bouquets like plain women who timidly answer a new mode. On the bare earth a thick viridian moss creeps up about the base of the solemn stones—moist and spongy; when a sunbeam strikes its carpet it gives off a fine breath of mounting steam.

For quite suddenly the long calendar of rainy days would admit a perfect interval of brilliant sunshine. The garden steamed and we left our wooden ark, to stretch and saunter in the damp shades of a tropical Ararat. Everywhere new busy pushing foliage, and some horrid visitants—a nameless insect in a big cocoon which had the gritty feel of the grey flue from a vacuum cleaner. It darted two legs and a wily neck, moving with obscene sloth on mysterious errands.

So much for the garden, if it could be called garden— the narrowest that ever bore the name, a mere embroidery on the central motif of the house, to which sooner or later we always returned, since it was cooler and more roomy than out-of-doors. A Japanese house in the warm weather, recently built, with new screens and fresh floor-coverings, has a prettiness, an air of elegant economy, that flatters different senses with the same skill. The sense of touch is pleased by sliding doors and windows, made of thin wood and obedient to the lightest pressure; while the sense of smell sums up in a single whiff the cleanly virgin quality of the entire fabric.

All maiden, all pristine and all scented; a perfume of sweet aromatic woods, sawn and polished when the little house was raised, and still redolent, strongly redolent, of their native virtues. The mats are scented; they are green when they are laid down and acquire their golden lustre with use and time. For the moment their greenness and newness strike the nostrils and they crepitate—but very softly—underfoot. They are resilient; each is a solid slab, supported at the edges but not in the middle, and yields perceptibly to the tread of those who cross it. The amount of energy thus saved in the Far East might be calculated by the remark of an English scientist who affirms that, as we stand upon the ground, the molecules bear us up by a combined hammering, 'with force equivalent to some ten stone weight. . . . We are being continuously and vigorously buffetted'—but for which we should sink gently through the floor.

Perhaps it is because the assault of vigorous molecules is at any rate deadened by a yielding floor that our new house, when we first trod its springy *tatami*, suggested a pavilion for gazing immortals in a Chinese picture rather than a small house in the squalid suburbs of a modern town. Celestial life receives its charm, one had always imagined, from the complete subservience of such matter as yet persists. There amid the vistas of the heavenly landscape one could realize one's dream of sinking through the ground, or standing knee-deep in the mirror-surface of a polished table; for the material world would be as dreamy as a tame cat, as pliant, as full of languorous inclinations—not the tigrish creature that carries us between its claws and deals out its perpetual admonitory buffets. . . .

The golden *tatami*, then, are a triumph of art, if one accepts the Japanese notion of how to exist. They combine comfort with a certain degree of austerity, and temper softness with a resilience that never flags. You can stand upon them, sit upon them or lie upon them; they demand care, and muffle footsteps throughout the house. They are a pleasant but also a respectable institution, and lend a ceremonious dignity to the meanest room. The touch of ceremony—here as elsewhere you cannot elude it—in Japan where vice itself is ceremonial. Everything that takes place upon the mats seems to draw from them a subdued overtone, an added suavity, which gives the servant presenting his accounts the air of a Minister and surrounds an aimless call with the importance of a state visit.

One had one's cue, and, if somehow one failed to recognize it, a Western upbringing was probably at fault. We have learned to dislike ceremonies in the remote West; we live untidily with loud laughter and frequent rages; we run in and out and bang the doors. While here the doors —those fragile canvas screens—slipped noiseless to and fro along their grooves; a lifted voice would penetrate the whole house, and in the street arrest gaping passers-by. . . . Two rooms, side by side upon the ground floor,

A CLASSICAL JAPANESE INTERIOR

looked forth on to the railway-carriage garden, its dead tree and further bank of glossy shrubs—two bare rooms, a double sliding-door between, with walls of some dark brown composition having a curious mica finish as rough as sandpaper, framed in smooth corner-posts of white wood. Grained planks overhead and narrow roof-joists completed the effect of living in a large box—a casket you could pull open to show the pigeon-holes or shut up tightly till no aperture was to be found.

For once the wooden shutters had been pushed home and securely bolted on the inside with a wooden pin, the house was as impregnable-looking and blank as during the daytime it had seemed welcoming and airy. Behind the shutters, stored away from dawn to dark in a deep slot like cards within their pack, were the glass screens, a Western innovation, and the translucent paper screens, which are called *shoji*, running on either side of the boarded verandah-passage. Otherwise there were no means of securing the house; and the Japanese, who live in constant terror of armed marauders, bolt themselves in firmly before going to bed, even on the hottest nights of the breathless season.

So the *amado* would be trundled from their slot and slammed heavily along their runners and into place, *slam-slam* all around us through the dark, as the glowing paper windows disappeared and the wonderful distorted shadows that fell across them. . . . *Shoji* are beautiful at any time, though quite useless if you expect them to give you shelter. At its newest the stretched rice-paper on the wooden frame—stretched by shrinking it with water from the mouth, which is absorbed and blown out in a fine cloud—tempts a finger as fresh snow tempts the feet.

It is taut and, should you flick it with a nail, the diaphragm will return a faint *ping!* White and clear, it coolly filters the hard sunshine and lets forth a warm radiance on to the dusk.

And the shadows! You suddenly notice a woman's coiffure like a looped sea-shell on the inside of a paper pane, as she stoops with extended neck towards her work, or the round head and prominent ears of a little boy. . . . An electric globe is far too brutal a projector to give these shadow-pieces the depth and delicacy they require. You need lamplight, its indeterminate pure shine, as a background for the enormous phantom shapes which dance and sway as the human actors move. . . . Nowadays, at least around the cities, every house has its blazing electric bulb; the houses like the people are in transition and still cast the old shadows with a new crudity.

Our own house had its fiercely powerful electric blaze; it had its glass screens and something else into the bargain —a small and chilly 'Western-style' room, across the entry from the matted apartments upon the left. A dismal feature it was and rather expensive—it raised the rent by a couple of pounds a month—though for a Japanese an undoubted gain in face, with its yellowish woodwork, its parquet floor and distempered walls which represented the very climax of modern luxury and afforded a fitting reception-room for important visitors. I have seen enough of such rooms in Japanese houses to be able to picture the furnishings that were its due; a round table, a plush cloth and a mammoth ash-tray, wicker chairs set about in a despondent circle, perhaps an oil-painting or a large and slippery oleograph, and an *art-nouveau* figure on a small bracket.

Le dernier cri! There we had it; and in these surroundings solemn parties, almost speechless, should have been held, the silent guests slightly inclined towards the centre, every face with its glassy-frigid smile, while the chit-chat began and then expired, flickered and died, flickered up and flickered out again, to a lulling cadence of sharp nervously drawn breaths. . . . I can see it now; but at that time the sepulchral chamber merely struck us as a bleak forbidding room which must be redone from top to bottom as soon as possible. Alas, the decorator, said a student who was interpreting for us, thought a dark blue wainscot wholly improper. Well, let him! . . . But I am anticipating, for our installation is a part of the story which has not yet found its peg, though it was momentous and full of drama while it lasted. Twenty students, with the best intentions in the world, had offered to devote their time to helping us, and had divided up their number into several shifts, each shift to spend a few hours beneath our roof.

We learned then the embarrassment of royal personages who cannot escape from their attentive retinue which presses around them. All day and every day of a sweltering week, our bodyguard was in attendance at the house, in a little cluster sitting upon the floor, smoking and talking softly among themselves. We wanted—but our wants were multifarious and, if few foreigners have ever wanted with such perversity, never were their hapless whims so gently humoured, though it often ended in a mild blink of mystification. Women don't give orders in Japan; or they give them in a somewhat deprecating way. They are malleable, not furious and determined, and, when the workman shakes his head over a projected colour, there is no

39

flare-up, no obstinate show of resistance, which affects the student as a downright impropriety. . . . On our part, besides the difficulty of language, there was the fact that a simple and brief request contained the germ of flowing paragraphs in Japanese, usually supplemented by the interposition of our own servant. He, too, had his ideas on the right colour; he, too, spoke at length while the others listened. Mad foreigners! All foreigners are mad; but the crazy duo eventually got its way. The splendid room was horribly repainted, and our bodyguard, somewhat shaken, took their departure, collecting caps and coloured kerchiefs, and the solid boots which they had shed upon the door-sill when they arrived.

First the siege, then the drama of the move; doubts of my real vocation became more ominous. I was left to turn them over and turn them round, in an aromatic wooden box under the rain or in a wooden bath alongside the tiny kitchen, where tradesmen were chattering noisily to the ancient cook. . . . Tradesmen's voices, hot water, clouds of steam—they have coalesced in my memory as a single impression. The bald cook could be heard talking to the grocer's boy, and the words 'Master' and 'Mistress', in Japanese, floated through with a significance I could not catch. These foreigners!—'butter-smelling fools', as a friend of ours once heard a man describe them. . . . Japanese conversation to a Western ear has an echo of the insect world in its monotonous rhythm; up and down, up and down the voices ramble, on and on, seldom varying their speed, in tones of pleasant reasonableness or mild annoyance.

Meanwhile, in the oval wooden bath, I enjoyed the peace which comes from immersion in very hot water and stared out through a muslin shroud of steam. I have already written of the bathroom at the hotel—our private bath was incomparably more soothing, an oval tub of upright wooden slats, bound with wire and fitted with a small stove which continued to heat the water after you had entered it. The new wood gave off a steamy fragrance; and the position which the shape of the bath required— sitting vertical, your hands around your knees, somewhat the posture of a child within the womb—was conducive to an equilibrium of body and spirit, often unattainable in those early months.

Every day would begin in the same manner; bath and tradesmen. . . . But then sometimes before the bath, sometimes even before the neighbours' *amado* had been shot back noisily along their grooves, I used to wake and find the garden beyond the fence lying becalmed below a clear but sunless sky. A shabby place as seen from our two bedrooms which occupied the upper storey of the house, it had a pond, usually empty, and a twisted pine, a willow-tree, a stone lantern and vague accessories, all a trifle dusty and out of repair. Arid and rather dejected by the light of day, in the dawn-light under an horizon as pale as glass it would be emerging, very remote but very distinct, from the transparent fast-evaporating dregs of shadow. Silence around the rim of the tumbled skyline seemed to be clamped down like a solid crystal bell, and the whole landscape beneath this smooth enormous concave quickened and expended slowly in subdued brightness. Then the pine-boughs, the strange hummocks of the earth, tall grass-spears and the dry pond with its greyish pebbles, had the quality half radiant and half dim of something observed through depths of untroubled water. A little apart from the other trees, against the sky, the willow drooped its sheer-descending foliage, long crane's feathers, the purest, softest emerald, which billowed at the approach of a morning breeze.

CHAPTER IV

INTERIOR

A vague breeze ruffling across the garden, while every object became heavier and more opaque; then noises, which started almost simultaneously, announced that life in the crowded neighbourhood had begun. Our own house slept later than the rest; but presently there was a hollow cough and the squeak of *amado*. We heard our servant who was moving about the rooms, lightly tickling the slumbrous furniture with a feather whisk.

Bent and ghostly in his ghostly crumpled robe, a cigarette clenched expertly between his teeth, on such occasions he was more than ever like a goblin—the huge ears, the wrinkled face and the bald skull—as he went shuffling web-footed to and fro. An ancient efrit whom we had summoned by magic arts and who was presently to vanish whence he had come; in the meantime an extremely serviceable familiar who cooked the meals, dusted the mats and ran our errands. . . .

Poor Hayashi San! His virtues recommended him; but it was his vices that made him impossible to forget. We had engaged him one afternoon in a friend's house, where

43

he had appeared and duly prostrated himself upon the floor, solemn as any djinn from the *Arabian Nights*, charming and venerable in his sober-coloured silk. How venerable, how benevolent! we had both exclaimed. The head of a Buddhist abbot carved in boxwood, for his skin was of a peculiar earthy brown and curiously seamed as by the gouging strokes of a clever chisel, which had dug deep scores on either side of his long upper lip and smoothly indented the conical hump of his hairless skull. An ascetic, one might have imagined at a first glance; but the traces left by high-thinking and loose-living are not always to be distinguished without difficulty—in point of fact, they have often been confused. And, though Hayashi San never quite lost his benevolence, our opinion of his ascetic qualities soon declined.

He had a secret. What it was, heaven knows; but it absorbed him, literally swallowed him, when his work was finished. He would flit away after a courteous goodnight with the observation that he was now going to take his bath, and till three o'clock or four o'clock of the early morning would not return to his thin mattress in the passage-room. The neighbouring bath-house closed its doors about eleven; at midnight the last trams disappeared. No sign; and then eventually the soft slither of his mattress being dragged across the floor, a stumbling sound, a low grunt, a stifled cough and Hayashi San had rolled over and gone to sleep. He would rise again, shaky but indomitable; he would amble with bent back on our commissions—a goblin figure, submissive and yet defiant, whom old age and hardening sinews could not tame, but who still travelled like a tom-cat through the darkness or shuffled home, lean and exhausted, towards his bed.

44

Strange and awful, should we catch him unexpectedly, was the face he sometimes showed as he opened the door —for example when we had been away during the week-end and came back without a telegram late on Sunday. He was ill, he muttered, apologizing for his nightgown; and he *was* ill, there could be no possible doubt of that, earthy-pallid, the crumpled cere-cloths which enveloped him giving forth a stale odour of the other world, an aged Lazarus—but it was not for Lazarus we had bargained when we interviewed the benevolent elder in the silk kimono.

'Hayashi San, what time did you go to bed?'

A pause. 'Half past eleven, Danna San.'

'How odd! Because at twelve I couldn't find you. . . .'

Not a syllable; but the long grisly wrinkled upper lip would be pulled taut over the prominent yellow teeth. The deaf adder had effectually shut its ears and would not listen to the mild music of friendly pleadings. . . .

We gave up; we were distressed but let him go; for the silence of a Japanese is hard to combat. It is dense; it is woolly and soporific. It says everything by saying no-thing and meaning nothing; and it descends like a ton-weight of feather bed, snowing down till opposition is blotted out. Thus already, during our first month in the new house, Hayashi's nocturnal habits became a rule. His work finished, he doffed his jacket and trousers for a second-best kimono and cloth cap; he said good-night and lit his cigarette, then shuffled away into the obscurity of the narrow lane.

Rather refreshing, in this unmysterious country, was the blot of mystery provided by his absence. Most of our friends preferred maidservants about the house—devoted creatures whose only pastime at odd moments was to comb and recomb their long hair in the tiny rooms of three-mats'-width in which they lived and where one usually caught sight of them upon entering, as they squatted beneath the unshaded electric globe. Too much hair, we had decided at a brief acquaintance. Yuki San— Miss Snow. Such a pretty name!—might be as angelic as her mistress liked to assume. We pictured the loose bundles of oily hair, and felt comfortable in our possession of the bald Hayashi.

For he had merits, was honest, so we considered; and, though his honesty, like all honesty, was merely relative, the alloy with which he brought it up to weight was interfused according to a strictly conventional plan. Here, as elsewhere, convention had been at work, rolling and levelling the various avenues of human life; and down these avenues, neatly sighted by ancient wisdom, our cook in perfect security could take his way. One must not cheat; to cheat is reprehensible. One may 'squeeze'; for to squeeze is not the same. Just as the rubber-grower makes the rounds of his plantation, opening little cuts in the living bark from which he draws off a regular drop of vegetable gold, so the squeezer extracts a regular small pittance from every source which he can tap without diminishing, from his master, from the tradesmen, even the errand boys—but the last expedient is not to be recommended; and if Hayashi San ever swerved from the straight path, it was his employers who had forced him from the crown of the road. . . .

The system in itself is not illogical; your expenditure is adjusted to your income, to your own sense—or the tradesmen's sense—of your financial stature. The bills of a First Secretary at a foreign embassy are, as a matter of course, larger than those of a Third. A foreign professor must submit to this classification; or his servant will lose face and look aggrieved. How aggrieved! He will limp sighing about the house, and squeeze the errand boys until they dare not approach the door. Then the delinquent will notice that a certain shop—though he telephones, almost begging for a delivery—seems never or very seldom to produce his purchases. He will be mystified till the arrival of a new servant suddenly and inexplicably removes the embargo.

In spite of these difficulties and disappointments Hayashi San continued with us seven months. Mr. Hayashi—our formality never flagged, and his willingness to do his best by us remained at par. 'Mr. Hayashi!'—and from the stifling slip of kitchen '*Hai-eee!*' came his response from near the stove. 'I am coming! What else should I do but come? A moment's patience!' The long-drawn despairing wail compressed an entire paragraph within itself, sometimes cheerful, sometimes strenuous and hard-driven, accompanied by a great clatter of dishes and saucepans. . . .

Like most servants, he accumulated nameless trifles, and this collection was apt to impede him while he worked, in a kitchen where at the best of times there was little elbow-room, barely space for a cupboard and a gas-stove, for a few shelves and a rickety wooden bench. It was on the bench that he sat down to read his newspaper and to smoke during the quiet of the afternoon, a crumpled tin near his hand which he used as ash-tray, and a yellow-green packet of cigarettes. In the hottest weather he would sit on the kitchen step, hanging his legs into the desolate backyard, and there sometimes receive parties of his friends, younger men who also worked for foreigners and brought with them the gossip of the English colony. Foreigners' servants are a separate corporation, a *rusé* and rather disreputable *haut ton*, enfranchised from the traditional loyalties of the domestic class, enjoying wider freedom and higher wages. Your servant knows everybody else's servant and exactly where you are invited and what you do. In his turn, he passes through the same channels some observations on your character and monetary standing.

But nothing is more marked in the Japanese character than its knack of balancing interest with genuine kindliness; and I should be doing poor Hayashi a grave wrong if I depicted his attitude as merely grasping. Of course he squeezed, but then it was his employer—and an employer who himself broke all the rules—while towards the individual, who lay beneath, he exhibited, failing sympathy, a rare tolerance. Thus he humoured, though it cost him a shake of the head, our fondness for the pair of kittens we had adopted and who ranged, squalling hungrily, about the house, when their legs were too weak almost to bear them. A pair of females. . . . We had heard a pitiful piping which seemed to come from a dislodged nestful of young birds and, opening the door, had found some urchins on the doorstep, carrying a large box of struggling kittens. Like pious Buddhists, they were on their way to expose the creatures, in any nook where they could be left to die of starvation—a method regularly followed by the Japanese, with now and then a pinch of food thrown in, uneatable but a formal acknowledgment of the right to live.

Even the ghost of an exposed kitten must be treated

properly, and, if so treated, may be relied upon to return the compliment. Our kittens, not yet resigned to a decorous fate, near a rubbish-heap, in a gutter or behind a fence, were piping and wriggling miserably within their prison, shrinking from the hard light and the fresh air, for they were probably not more than three weeks old. We picked out two; the others were sent away towards a destiny which it is better to leave obscure—two kittens so weak they could hardly stand, sprawling on faint legs across the floor and creeping away into corners from the sunshine. They plucked up courage; they learned to suck a milky rag, and developed all the energy of plebeian natures—common cats, as our acquaintances pointed out, bob-tailed mongrels with very little in their favour except the charm of youth and feline liveliness.

Saint-Évremont, that pleasant writer and agreeable man, used to observe in the closing years of his life that 'when we grow old and our own spirits decay, it reanimates one to have a number of living creatures about one, and to be much with them'. Our spirits, though not definitely on the decline, certainly flagged at this period as seldom before; and the only remedy against depression which never failed was the noisy presence of a pair of growing cats. For me in the companionship of dogs there will always be something a trifle harrowing, as in the mute tenderness of a simple-minded younger brother; while a cat's temperament, so voluptuous and yet so frigid, is as good to contemplate as its steel spine and electric coat—its quick spurts of affection and blazing indifference that wax and wane with the slotted pupils in the golden iris. . . . Their vitality—every game was a mimic battle, and into every posture the same dispassionate energy flowed. Even sleep appeared an energetic function which tensely occupied every muscle and every nerve, and recalled by contrast the whimpering sleep of dogs. We love cats for their unlikeness to ourselves—the noblest, least vulgar reason for loving; our love resembles Spinoza's love of the Divinity in as much as it does not hope for any return. . . .

They were alive, and the constant spectacle of life and energy glittered through the background like a metallic thread, when rain was falling or vapour rising beyond the windows. To watch them was to feel oneself awake; and for two months now, ever since we landed at Kobe, real life had worn a curious dreamy cast, which in the end we became accustomed to and scarcely noticed. Landscape, climate and the people they have matured—all seemed to be labouring beneath an incantation that hung down as low and heavy as the sky, and somehow blunted the fine edge of daily experience. As in Lotosland it was always afternoon, juicy and overripe with rain on the breeze; but the lotos-food itself was lacking in savour and, while we chewed it, had a watery acrid taste. During the weeks which were spent by us at the hotel, we had sometimes tried to eat Japanese dishes, and found the experience diverting rather than pleasurable. Very pleasurable for the eye it undoubtedly was, to see the lacquer trays set out by a kneeling maid, the covered soup-bowls, the big red-lacquer rice-tub, the porcelain bottle of warm and fragrant rice-wine and the porcelain cup like an egg-shell broken in half. . . . A charming still-life; the pink slivers of raw fish side by side with opalescent cubes of bean-curd, set off by the bright discs of yellow pickle and a varied assortment of dark browns and oily greens, among red and black lacquer and blue earthenware.

But the Western palate—later, the Western stomach—
did not confirm the pleasure of the eye; most dishes were
so insipid as to be nearly tasteless, while some few possessed a horribly haunting tang that, once tasted, it was
difficult to forget; thus *daikon,* the strongly smelling
pickled radish, inclined to hang like garlic upon the
breath, and edible seaweed in a thin and bitter soup where
pale prawns floated with vegetable debris. . . . Nor did the
rice-wine, to which I had ingenuously looked forward,
deserve the slender flask in which it appeared or the delicate ribbed cup from which I drank it. The bottle and the
cup were above reproach; the amber fluid was pleasantly
warm but tasted muddy; it included the second-cousins of
several flavours, Amontillado, flat beer and stagnant
pond-water. . . .

Tastes ranged from the haunting to the wholly indefinite, the indefinite being in a considerable majority; and
the odours, which formed the background of our life,
were vague and clinging more often than strongly pungent. Crowds here, to take an instance, did not smell, if
one escaped a sudden nauseous stench of *daikon* and the
acrid fume of *Shikishima* cigarettes. The streets had a not
unpleasing distinctive odour, if one ignored a waft of
sewage and dirty soapsuds and, in the summer time, of a
rank sweetish disinfectant which is used in the open cess-
pit of every house. . . . Nature, too, supplied an occasional
violent perfume, but on the whole preferred odours which
were somewhat toneless—such as the scent of a certain
flowering tree, whose seminal fragrance, sticky and low-
lying, made the rainy dusk yet closer and more prison-
like.

Lilies were an exception to this rule. In July they are the commonest cut flower, and for a shilling we could purchase them in great swathes, huge reddish blooms with turned-back yellow petals boldly flecked like the petals of an English tiger-lily, each fleck slightly raised on the waxen ground and the entire petal faintly crimped as though by curling-tongs. Their size, the waxen thickness of their substance, the long pistils heavily clotted with red pollen, gave every head a look of fierce intensity that suited the violent perfume they distilled, delicious, blatant and enervating in the same breath:

> *Il est des parfums frais comme des chairs d'enfants,*
> *Doux comme les hautbois, verts comme les prairies,*
> *Et d'autres, corrompus, riches et triomphants,*
>   *Ayant l'expansion des choses infinies. . . .*

Rich and triumphant and corrupt, the lilies flared like music across the room. In a universe of half-tones and subtle hints, they were as gratifying as a strong light under the sea.

CHAPTER V

STREET SCENE

How often we asked ourselves if we were awake—that question which one may ask but never answer! We looked to the outer world for re-assurance. It was more dreamlike and inconsequent than the world within. . . .

A steep lane dipped crazily past our door, dividing us from the chocolate-painted girls' school, a 'Western-style' frame-building of great size, with the blear aspect of any public institution. From our hotel bedroom we had sometimes watched its boarders, and now they in their turn could watch us—an opportunity of which they immediately took advantage and continued to profit by as long as we remained in Tokyo. After a year our magnetism was still as strong and, should we try sitting in the garden or near the screens, our mere presence would attract in the opposite windows a dark cluster of interested heads. Round faces, thick dangling glossy pigtails, a subdued buzz and occasionally a timid voice: '*Neko!* *Neko!*' imitating my way of calling the cats, or more satirically: 'Poo-us! Poo-us!' which broke down into a storm of helpless giggles.

Among themselves they were infinitely polite, and the slip of lane between our door and the school-entrance resounded to their ceremonious goodbyes: *Sayonara! Sayonara!* as they left the building and bade a sibilant farewell to dawdling friends. . . . Below the school there were a number of little shops, a printer's, an embroiderer's, a clog-shop; then the alley met a somewhat broader thoroughfare which climbed at a gentle slope towards the crossroads.

That street was typical of the modern Tokyo—not of its main arteries, mushroom offices and towering department stores, but of the Tokyo which lies always around the corner, an easy stone's throw from the bright lights and the grinding trams. Vague and slatternly, a sprawling skyline of wooden houses overlooked by a massive procession of telegraph poles that marched—or rather staggered—up its slope, linked together by loose wires in a drooping curve. . . . These telegraph poles, as though conscious of their superiority, never take the trouble to stand straight. Like street bullies, their hands deep in their pockets, they lurch drunkenly over the cowering shabby roofs and lean at affected angles on strong supports. The old Japan is changing in their shadow; the future belongs to them and all they symbolize. The squalor of the new 'progressive' city has the effect of a perpetual sardonic sneer.

And yet, beneath the avenue of lurching poles, there was a curious ch :m in the little shops that lined the street. The restaurant—it was the old-fashioned Japanese restaurant as it is illustrated in the travel scenes of Hiroshige, with its awning made of printed cotton strips and charming display of a few carefully chosen bowls. Even a cheap restaurant must do its best to appear well-bred; and the pickles or the slices of raw fish were set out on beautiful blueish earthenware and decorated with a jagged frill of green. The seal-cutter's—such shops are in every street and show select examples of the workman's handiness, soapstone cubes topped by a miniature Chinese lion, globes of crystal and squares of syenite or onyx. There were grocers, there were barber's shops and fishmongers; and, as in most countries, the piles of fish were worth examining; live eels, which seethed in a wooden tub and were nailed down and skinned while a customer waited, flaccid cuttlefish, the terra-cotta limbs of octopi, spidery crabs with prickling pear-shaped shells, red mullet and blue enormous tunny.

The shop-boys, like young aquatic gods, sported amid this profusion of marine life, scraped and flayed, paddling cheerfully to and fro. Further on was a large and dusky shop where bouquets of parchment flowers were being woven, funeral flowers, stiff bunches of white lotus arising from a diminutive china vase. Completed bunches, three and four feet high, with large pointed buds and round leaves, shone ghostly in the darkness of upper shelves; while over the shop-front a swift had built her nest, undisturbed and unafraid, on a tiny bracket.

She swooped low down across the street and fluttered in towards her fledglings under the eaves. A noisy street; its surface was rough and pebble-strewn, and cars nosed through cautiously from the main road, the occupants at the back jolting and swaying. Bicycles, much bolder than the cars, came swerving with desperate speed from left to right, ridden by errand boys who wore suits of cotton underclothes, jaunty caps, loin cloths and rubber boots, and tinkled their bell insistently as they worked the pedals. Very often there shot past upon a bicycle a boy who was balancing single-handed an entire collation in a pyramid of lacquer trays, riding furiously but never losing his equilibrium, though he tacked with dangerous sharpness among the throng.

A crowd here was like no crowd in Europe or, for that matter, in the other countries of the Far East, slow-moving, talkative and self-important, with a curious zig-zag progress all its own. A Western crowd twinkles like grains of quicksilver, the chance assemblage of rapidly moving individuals; Japanese form a heavy and viscous stream, bobbing and shuffling with a great air of common activity, though its separate units may in fact be completely aimless. They walk slowly when they appear to be walking fast; they are most idle when apparently most busy. Born *flaneurs*. . . . The cumbrous wooden clog clacks with a leisurely movement from side to side, only secured by a leather thong next the big toe and not conducive to a brisk and forward gait. Young elegants, loosely girt in summer kimono, workmen in tight trousers and dark blue coolie-coats, their employer's crest stamped largely across the fabric, street-sellers, students and modern business men, all describe the same vague and rambling course. They do not jostle; there is a nervous shrinking from physical contact, an air of guarded good behaviour and slight constraint. Even the loud laughter of a group of hobbledehoys rings untrue, as it were deadened, a trifle pathetic.

And then the children. . . . The narrow street was full of children, among whom their elders gently picked their way—boy-children in sailor suits or wadded robes, and

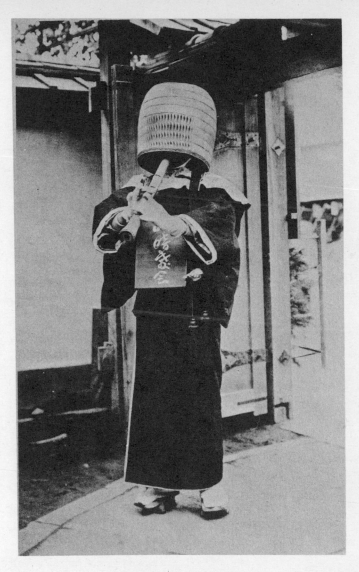

A STREET MUSICIAN
IN THE COSTUME OF A BEGGING PRIEST

little girls who deferred to the little boys. The boys were already budding tyrants, who never forgot that they were males and the pride of a family; while the girls, with their black-slitted olive masks, were just awaking to the subservient role of womanhood, but were still pretty, still agile and unabashed, though they knew better than to contradict their little brothers.

Street merchants often appeared in the crowded fairway, collecting all the children around their carts—the man who blew a continuous stream of bubbles, tiny and iridescent, from a tube-shaped pipe, men who peddled sweet-stuff and paper toys, and once a man who dealt in living frogs, emerald green, the diameter of a sixpenny piece, conveniently attached to cotton threads. Among the children who gathered round for the entertainment were larger girls with babies on their backs, stooping beneath the weight of the immobile infant which gazed out, goggling and tearless, from under the coat that enveloped both the nursemaid and her charge. Great boobies these perambulators in human form, as they shuffled at a snail's pace from show to show—indefatigable audience of a moving theatre where the foreigners from up the street gave a favourite turn.

Entering a shop to buy a button or a box of matches, we would notice that the air had become quite dark, and then glance up and see the window packed with onlookers. Japanese inquisitiveness is constitutional. Neither friendly nor unfriendly, it is simply indifferent. In country districts, I am told by those who have lived there, dense throngs accompany the foreigner on the smallest errand; and in Tokyo, where foreigners are by no means scarce, they still arouse deep wonder at every step.

They are *so* strange, so utterly inhuman—heaven knows we began to agree with our silent audience; we must indeed be strange, we privately mused, caught on the fly-paper of that tense unwinking scrutiny which seemed to annihilate any pretension to personal life.

Somewhat baffled and short of temper, we moved away and left behind us the long upward-sprawling street, its two-storeyed shops beneath the telegraph poles—indeterminate and confused in the hardest sunshine. Japanese towns have no redeeming sense of space, no straight vistas nor sudden suggestions of wealth and elegance; but rich and poor huddle together cheek by jowl, and the beautiful, where it exists, is hidden from sight among objects the least calculated to betray its secret. Nowhere is the incongruous so little shunned; I have felt at times that it was deliberately cultivated for the sake of contrast. Even the trees are surrounded with hideous crutches, and their limbs and boles deformed by clumsy overcoats.

All is charmless, all dishevelled at a first glance—the deep gutters choked with stagnant dishwater, the dreary wooden fences and the blind gates. Such charm as there is must be coaxed out gradually, like a perfume which only develops from use and handling. Our quarter was one of many in the modern town, and every quarter, beside its broad and bustling streets, includes a labyrinth of narrow muddy lanes with temples, myriad shops and steaming bath-houses. Here are the makers of native instruments, of bamboo flutes and of the long-necked graceful *samisen* that geisha play, its pegs slanting as cleverly as the pins in their coiffure; the pawnshops, the carpenters, the umbrella-and-clog shops, the shops where paper lanterns are covered and stencilled. You could walk for hours; but in the end there is little variety and Hongo and Kojimachi seem much alike. Separate districts rarely possess a separate character; but the whole city is a huge extension of a single neighbourhood, swarming and unplanned and out at elbows, tumbled roofs and peeling fences mile on mile.

Ancient graveyards are wrapped away in the city's folds, half engulfed by the scabby growth of modern houses. I remember one; we had wandered in from a noisy street and along a paved passage under a gate, then round on broken flags behind a temple amid a forest of stone cylinders, specked with moss, which sprang up between the dusty colourless tree-trunks. A silent, dim and melancholy place; the obelisks were still attended and kept in repair, but the impression of age and neglect was very strong. Was the shape of these cylindrical stones phallic, and what was the meaning of these thin laths stuck in the ground, bunched untidily at the feet of the newer monuments? What did they mean—the rudimentary stone figures with the red bibs stitched around their necks? I was almost glad to hear the murmur of distant trams, like the noise of the sea in the depths of a dusty conch.

About the temples there was something still alive, for the superstitions of different periods need not clash, and the very old had come to terms with the very new. The fox-shrines were always pleasant to visit in passing—the shrines, that is to say, of the Shinto Rice Spirit who is confused with his pair of tutelary foxes. The fox is a ghostly animal in Japanese legend, a wizard who has the power of changing his shape and imposes himself on peasants and lonely travellers, tapping the tip of his brush against the door.

An acquaintance, who is fond of solitary walks, once described to us how he had reached a mountain cottage and *tapped*, hoping for shelter and a bed, whereas a Japanese would have pushed open the sliding door. The inmates, at first unwilling to answer the summons, appeared at length haggard and discomposed. He was not admitted till they had walked carefully round him, peering for the tell-tale tip of the fox's brush.

So the Inari foxes on pedestals before a shrine raise their brushes with a knowing defiant stiffness and from pointed snouts seem always to be smelling the breeze—an embodiment of the malicious streak in nature, of the cunning resistance that we discover in the heart of things, the unaccountable swiftly changing demons of luck. They are benevolent, too, and now and then a scarlet bib is tied across the chest of a friendly fox. There are foxes large and small, in stone and bronze, the arrogant renard and the playful vixen amid her cubs, a dozen foxes on pedestals in the same compound where the leaves are swept up and the children play and suppliants pause an instant to clap their hands, with a form of worship at least as sensible as many others.

Whether the Japanese are at heart 'a religious race', it is happily not my business to try to decide. They are superstitious—as all races more or less—with the racial sense of propriety into the bargain, their feeling for law and order in both worlds, an inclination to do as they hope to be done by. A traveller who, like myself, comes and goes, can only remark that religious feelings are unobtrusive and, when they appear, assume a clannish and sociable cast perfectly consonant with other traits he may have observed. Every function is a function of public life and

demands for its performance a social setting. Secretive as
they may appear when the shutters are drawn, at moments they are gregarious to the point of childishness.

They love—one feels they need—to be together; and
the great charm of existence in a crowded neighbourhood
is reflected from the steady flow of its common life; families who sit in the background of the small shops,
wielding fans or on cold days poking the brazier, and the
warmth and animation which surrounds the bath-house
where they soak and scrub promiscuously side by side. A
little gaiety! It can be squeezed from almost anything, a
scrap of gossip which, in hot water and clouds of steam,
may expand like one of those withered paper blossoms
which they manufacture for the street-vendors of the remote West. On summer evenings the lane that passed our
door would be enlivened by young men returning home,
from the bath-house in which they had wound up the
day's affairs. Through the dusk, warm and moist as a
soothing compress, misty with the blurred gold of an
electric lamp, the pale bath-robes came wavering down
the slope, wooden clogs dully accompanying the rhythm
of speech, in laughing loquacious knots of two and three
—to thin and vanish before the watchman started his
rounds.

CHAPTER VI

THE MODERN CITY

A different world opened in the modern thorough-fares, all the stranger for its resemblance to the world we knew: trams, thundering lorries and hooting taxi-cabs. Here the little low-browed Japanese shops, with their cavernous fronts and small barred upper windows, had assumed a vertical mask of hammered tin which imitated—unsuccessfully—stone or concrete. From every other shop along the pavement a loud-speaker, announcing the scores of the latest baseball match, trumpeted or wailed into the street; and huge signs, *T. Sasaki Trousers-Presser* and *K. Ito Flesh Fruits Store*, proclaimed the majestic advance of 'Western learning'.

It must be admitted that the ability to speak English seldom or never went with an English sign; but the face-value of such notices was all important. Hongo is built upon a rise, and, viewed from above, the populous districts around its feet resemble an untidy litter of tin boxes, some new, some battered and stained with rust. Further off, buildings in solid masonry, seven-storey offices and large banks, mark the commercial centre of the modern city; while the steep macadam road which plunges downhill, bisecting Kanda, the street of second-hand book-shops, leads past its mystic centre, the Imperial Palace, hidden away behind a ring of fortified moats.

These broad moats, the curving glacis they defend, the white corner-turrets and the bulk of a distant gate-tower, are one of the few beautiful prospects in the whole metropolis—*immediately* beautiful; but, even here, squalid out-buildings can be seen peeping over the wall and a chimney, the smoke-stack of the electric light plant, raises unreproved its sooty column. It was before the main gate of the palace enclosure that I had witnessed, soon after our arrival, perhaps the saddest and strangest procession I had ever imagined. My taxi had been held up by a crowd and a little policeman, in white knickerbockers and black puttees, a sword clashing fiercely about his calves, ordered the doltish driver to back his car and to shut and keep shut the pair of windows. It was a hot day, and for twenty or thirty minutes I sat expectant in the closed and stifling vehicle. The crowd, which lined the approach on either side, remained silent, with downcast eyes, also waiting; and gendarmes, their faces turned to the onlookers, watched them as a sheepdog watches sheep.

Not a sound; and then suddenly from the palace gate two motor cycles and sidecars went dashing by; then others, then a car containing officers, and at last, strictly escorted by police motor cycles, a long hearse-like limousine, of which the roof was decorated by four glistening silver knobs. The Imperial family; a flash of uniforms and ostrich feathers; but the crowd did not lift their eyes towards the car and the eyes of the policemen never left the silent crowd. No cheering; the Imperial car rushed by and disappeared down the avenue which leads to the railway station. Slowly, as if waking from a stupor, the crowd replaced their hats and began to move. . . .

The little mild descendant of the Sun was on his way to the red-brick railway station round the corner, from which in theory he alone can travel first, with his family and the princes of the blood—Emperor, *pontifex maximus*, commander-in-chief. The same dense silence accompanies him wherever he goes, the same breathless hush and stifling reverence. The subject of the Emperor and the Imperial family is rarely touched in conversation by the Japanese. It is too sacred—incidentally, too dangerous, for the suspicions of the political police are easily roused.

Within sight of the ramparts of the Imperial palace stands the hotel, built by an eccentric American architect, where tourists stay and dinner parties are often given. A queer façade, its pretentious squat asymmetry recalls a modernist chest-of-drawers in stone and brick, the stone used being of a repellently porous type, pocked with large holes like a Gruyère cheese. Inside it is dark and intricate as a feverish dream, and there are many passages in which one must stoop or bump one's head. A Japanese orchestra wails sugared American dance tunes or improvises on the ghost of a Scottish air. At the bookstall charming bright-eyed American matrons buy postcards or little handbooks to the Tea Ceremony, while their husbands, absorbed in the financial news, rustle intently through the heavy pages of American newspapers. Here also were the local English sheets; and from these one learned that the enterprising Tokyo geisha were taking up classes in 'Western eroticism' to compete with the more progressive café waitresses; that 'Premier Hamaguchi' had left his bed after 'the unfortunate occurrence' of a month ago—when a youthful patriot wounded him in the stomach.

Behind the hotel, which is expensive and well kept, electric trains roared along an embankment, and, through the railway arch, one came on a fetid canal, black and oily, with anchored barges full of rubbish. A minute's walk brought one to the Ginza, the nervous centre or spinal cord of the modern city, and the only street where its existence is truly urban and a drab suburban atmosphere does not prevail. A wide street, it is noisy and always crowded, though its destination and point of origin are equally vague. In its midmost stretch are gathered the large shops and the greatest confluence of people, trams and cars.

No wonder that the Japanese admire it. The long seclusion in which their history began has left them with a taste for noise and tumult that even the Ginza and its crowds and vehicles can hardly satisfy. Everything has been done to increase the uproar; the noise of traffic, continuous and quite deafening, is helped out, should a momentary lull impend, by the jangling bells of the paper-sellers on the kerb. Each newsvendor carries a cluster of little bells which he shakes without pause till his stock is exhausted. Here, too, there is a loud-speaker in every shop which pours forth its throaty blast across the pavement—baseball results, a lesson in English, a Japanese ditty—no matter; mere noise for the love of noise; while the dense crowd, well pleased if a trifle stupefied, moves shuffling to and fro in an endless stream.

The crowd itself proved eminently worth studying, for it contained various ingredients of the new Japan, which ranged from the revolutionary to the stolid and respectable. First of all, there were burgess-wives out shopping, subdued and somewhat dingy in greys and browns, bearing European reticules and cheap umbrellas, accompanied very often by a widowed mother-in-law whose white hair was cropped short like a little boy's and who pattered with painful obstinacy in her daughter's track. Japanese women, subordinate during youth, gain authority as strength and charm decline. The Japanese mother-in-law is a dreaded figure; and in these old women, bent and faltering, with rheumy lids, their scalps showing yellow through the whitish bristles, one seemed to recognize the revengeful grasp of age. The crayfish in Japan is a symbol of longevity; it has the rounded back of an ancient woman and also her claws. . . .

Since the Ginza is the busiest part of Tokyo, there were coats and trousers and straw hats wherever one looked. The Japanese have been encouraged to adopt the notion that European dress is essentially businesslike and more practical than the easier native garb, though a single glance at such a crowd would suggest the reverse. Collars gall them; waistcoats and tailored trousers crease awkwardly on muscular thighs and prominent stomachs. The characteristic straddling walk that suits them best is hideously incommoded by clumsy boots.

But Western clothes *mean* something in Japanese life, and for this reason must be endured however comfortless. The wearer has attained to a certain position, is an office worker, a petty official, a minor business man. The Japanese are not a realistic race, but prone to fetch their motives from the world of fantasy; and the trousered business men who scuttle along the streets carry the imprint of a dream upon their brows—a modern hustling Paladin every one, with an Eversharp and an American fountain-pen very conspicuous in the breast pocket of his coat, a wrist-watch, a straw hat and a leather brief-case which appears to bulge with Lord knows what important papers. . . .

A game, then; but, of course, in deadly earnest. No joking matter, this whirlpool of harsh sounds, this conglomeration of many-storeyed buildings and the strange types which they disgorged at every step. There were workmen and respectable *bourgeoisie*—a sober-coloured, steady moving stream, while on its surface drifted the scum of modern life, indicating a profound disturbance beneath its flow. The *mobo* and his female counterpart, the *moga*, in other words the modern boy and the modern girl, flaunted rather pathetically for all to see, marched up and down and dawdled and gossiped, as though they needed the reassurance of lights and noise, fearful lest in solitude they might evaporate.

The *mobo* was the complete American 'college boy', reconstructed with immense care from the current movies, but like most reconstructions a little lifeless. Flapping trousers, belted pullover and bow-tie—mimetically it was a brilliant piece of work; but the detail was more satisfying than the general effect. The *moga*, alas, was hampered by nature; a thousand years of squatting upon the mats has rounded the shin-bone of the Japanese leg, and the long limbs, high waists and slender flanks, that have inspired, if they do not always accompany, Western modes, form an assemblage seldom realized by Japanese womanhood.

Pathetic *moga*! Still, their carriage was sharp and brazen; they dabbed boldly at their shrinking faces with Western cosmetics, wore berets and silk hosiery and linked their arms, strolling up and down before the shops, miniature heroines who must be 'cute' if it cost their lives—as it cost, indeed, the little charm they had ever possessed. . . . I have seen exceptions: a certain *beauté du diable* sometimes flowered from the very impudence of the imposture, a face which was less a face than a painted mask, coarse in grain, sullen looking and rather animal, between two licked-down crescents of straight hair.

They were bold, with a timidity beneath the boldness, and their companions walked beside them with a brittle swagger, affording a curious tableau of modern youth, carefree, exempt from the ancient servitude, the old Japan securely dead beneath their heels—French heels, the rubber heels of American sports shoes. . . . Yet the old Japan, a ghost upon the air, could be felt, though it was buried and out of sight. Ice-cream parlours, fruitarian restaurants, shining pastry cooks—to me, at least, they never carried conviction. The display they made was cheerful, vulgar and noisy; but I seemed to divine a yawning gulf of inner emptiness.

They wanted. . . . The measure of modern vulgarity was the measure of a need which could not be satisfied. 'I want! I want!' proclaimed the resplendent soda fountains, all shimmering whiteness and polished metal, with assistants in white aprons and white caps energetic and loud-voiced behind the counter. As the want became progressively more agonizing, so did the vulgarity in which it vented itself become more blatant. Japan, I have sometimes thought in the flaring Ginza, had begun to suffocate in the coils of a deadening system many years before the 'black ships' first arrived—a system as pertinacious and remote from life as the stooping crones, with reddened eyelids and shrivelled cheeks, who still terrorize the younger women in a Japanese family. The West may have forced itself upon the East, but its impact corresponded to a growing need. Western 'materialism' may have destroyed an ancient culture, yet it fell like rain from heaven on a thirsty soil. . . .

And that old life, is it effectively dead and buried? Magniloquent reforms have taken place. There is a Diet where the members come to blows, a police force which cudgels socialists and harries students. There are universities and newspapers, schools and railways; and yet freedom, in the wider sense, is still a shadow. Political freedom, of course, is not to be looked for; and individual freedom, if it exists, springs up in such feeble spurts as these—the laughter of the modern boy and modern girl, flashy bars, garish cafés and syrupy cocktails.

Cafés are a typical feature of modern Tokyo and have developed like an epidemic in recent years, a rash spreading from the main streets to the murky alleys, from the capital to the lesser provincial towns. A café is any coign or cubby-hole which will accommodate three or four haggard waitresses, some rickety tables and chairs and a tiny bar. Dignified as the *Poppy* or as the *Hollywood*, as the *Sans Souci*, the *Select* or the *Mon Ami*, their decorations are usually in the 'modern style', with oddly designed furniture and triangular windows. Little cramped rooms, their lurid coloured lights, vitreous green, dull red or aching blue, cut a series of satanic crevices in a shadowy back street; passing by, one catches sight of the dumpy ministrants as they entertain a customer or wind the gramophone.

In some cafés the waitresses are all *moga*; in others they wear kimono and the high-piled coiffure, and sit at your table beneath a bough of blossoming cherry, made of paper and hung with coloured lamps. In both instances, their demeanour is free and forward, and they have heavily carmined lips and gold-stopped teeth. The gramophone is never allowed a rest; the customers laugh and talk with a favourite girl, who pours the sweetish sticky Japanese beer. A craving for the *louche*, for the unconventional is satisfied by these ministrants and these surroundings. This breath of sophistication and knowing modernity gives an adventure with a café waitress an added charm.

Not that the modern café is primarily a brothel. Many cafés are said 'to have upper rooms; but the paternal police, who insert a finger here as elsewhere, command that no waitress shall quit the premises till some time after the last customer has taken his leave. Assignations are, therefore, the general rule; and, when a cashier is reported to have robbed a bank, it usually transpires that a waitress is among his luggage. For amorists, in the middle and lower grades of society, they represent the modern Fata Morgana. Each café is a small Circean islet. . . .

More innocent and more amusing are the various cinemas. Japanese cinemas we did not visit very often, since one witnessed there either interminable domestic dramas or heroic films, with much sword-play and a rambling plot, beautifully photographed but tedious and hard to follow. I am thinking of the cinemas which showed Western films, talkies at which the teller in his box vociferated against the voice of the American star, rendering the rapid dialogue to the Japanese audience who sat open-mouthed beneath the screen, as it flickered with enormous heroine or gigantic hero. . . . We are so accustomed to the queer elysium of the darkened cinema that its quintessential strangeness escapes our notice. How odd, if one imagines oneself a Japanese newly introduced to the magic of a full-blown talkie, to sit entranced under the spell of a mighty face, to watch a vastly magnified human body, lips that open, teeth that flash and limbs that move, platonic sensualist in the shadow of a Titan charmer.

Comme aux pieds d'une reine un chat voluptueux. . . .

In their choice of pleasures, as in everything they do, the Japanese are both conservative and adaptable. Picture shops along the Ginza and other streets display postcards of Greta Garbo and Marlene Dietrich among the portraits of famous courtesans and popular wrestlers. Geisha-music is still to be heard on the wireless and gramophone, but theme songs travel like wildfire from mouth to mouth, and the appearance of a film by René Clair had set the errand boys whistling a tune: *Sous les toits de Paris*, as they swerved past.

How much more powerful—if you remove the cob-webs of false sentiment—is the sorcery exercised by the modern cinema than any spell in the repertoire of the Ancient East. The cinema is a sumptuous witches' cave, and here, whether it is in China or Japan, the modern Oriental loves to sit, warming his ennui at the cold fires of lunar magic. The cinema gives light but scarcely warmth; it is compounded of hollow illusions and false hopes, sending its audience away a little exhausted, after this glimpse of fabulous luxury and unknown freedom, out again into the dark and muddy streets.

Cinemas close early in Japan and, on leaving the com-fortable theatre and modern audience, there was still time to try another sort of amusement—to 'do a Ginza-walk' as the Tokyo people say. The Ginza is busy to a late hour,

71

for, after the shops have shut at six or seven, the night-stalls are erected in a long avenue, perhaps half a mile of them, big and small, with flaring electric globes beneath the awnings and the goods they vend arranged neatly on wooden shelves: gyroscopes, buzzing mechanical toys, knife-cleaners, coat-hangers and cheap watches; stalls that deal in such nostrums as powdered snake, which is bought for its aphrodisiac virtues, and are garlanded with sere bunches of dried frogs.

It was during the summer that we first performed a Ginza-walk, and, at that season, there were glow-worms to buy as pets, singing crickets and musically croaking frogs. An entire stall was devoted to cricket-cages, some square and plain and some ornate, circular red-lacquer palaces with tiny bars. In front of the stalls, a steady moving stream of onlookers pushed up and down the broad pavements, gathering densely round any point of interest, for example round the *go* players at their table. *Go*, an elaborate form of draughts, is played out of doors in the warm weather, under a single light, dangling from a wire which streaks with shadow the serious faces above the board. A dull game—or so it seems to a casual Westerner —it provides an excuse, none the less, for stopping and gazing. The Tokyo crowd are considered by other Japanese, by the more conservative citizens of commercial Osaka, as a bohemian higgledy-piggledy lot, with their Ginza-strolls and kindred modern pleasures. Certainly the Ginza at this hour reveals an amiable side of the Tokyo temperament, its easy-going loose-belted sociability which expands under the influence of the famous thoroughfare.

Home at the best of times is apt to be comfortless. It

is the haunt of domestic duty, of wife and children. In the surrounding lanes, already almost silent, the *soba* merchant trudges, pushing his barrow, stocked with steaming maccaroni for a late meal, and tootles a small melancholy horn. Amusement must be sought in the main streets, at the bath-house or in a modest game of *go*. There is Asakusa, the large and garish amusement park, and, beyond, the brilliant streets of the Yoshiwara.

CHAPTER VII

JOY QUARTER

The Joy Quarter, though its tariff charges are high, is not patronized by people of wealth and breeding. It is not 'smart', and the undoubted elegance, which is its keynote, has been provided in deference to the popular taste. Even Vice here. . . . But the word loses its value, where no discredit is attached to the role of whore and no shame attends the satisfaction of a physical impulse. A sense of shame has never distinguished the Japanese; and it has needed the corroding effect of Western literature and the slow infiltration of Christian doctrine to associate a bodily need and an ethical lapse. However, both poisons are hard at work, and modern Japanese may soon experience the pleasures of sinning. . . .

But not yet; there was nothing furtive about its atmosphere when our taxi pulled up at the main entrance and we dismounted and walked through into a wide street, past the policeman who stood sentry in his box. Broad and brilliant were the avenues which stretched beyond, with lofty houses in the traditional Japanese style, far loftier and more splendid than the usual house. . . . Rather empty; wheeled traffic is not allowed, and a curious hush weighed upon the spirit. A certain tension seemed to isolate the strolling groups, as though each loiterer were imprisoned in his own desire.

Since the Yoshiwara comprises a whole neighbourhood, there were restaurants, shooting galleries and little shops scattered in the long vistas of palatial brothels. Business was very bad at that time, and the doorkeepers, as they caught sight of foreign tourists, encouraged and harangued from where they sat, indicating the lighted arcade in front of the building. It was in this arcade that, during a less self-conscious period, the *joro* used to be exhibited behind bars. To-day only their photographs can be examined, set out like museum specimens in a glass case.

We must have looked at thirty or forty photographs, always with a growing sense of dismay. That a visitor could deliberately *choose* between such faces seemed as strange as that a fancier of exotic bulbs could deduce their colour and rarity from the earthy onion. Formless masks —a thick coat of *o shiroi* robbed their features of the last gleam of human significance, their bodies mere elaborate silk cocoons swaddled and compressed by a stiffened sash.

Besides photographs, the doorway of each brothel usually contained some single ornament or shrub arranged with conscious artistry to left or right—a dwarf pine, a flowering bush of azalea, sometimes a plaster cat on a small cushion, a 'welcome-cat' lifting its paw to greet the guests, even a bronze. . . . But there was no end to such refinements, and after wandering up and down in the hard light, pursued by the barking voices of eager doormen, we turned in at a large building on a main street, whence many servants rushed forward to receive us.

Inside was the same air of sober æstheticism. The dark boards glistened speckless underfoot, while the sliding doors, which shut off rooms on either side, were dappled and faintly spotted with pleasing patterns. The room, into which they showed us at the end of the corridor, was diminutive but appointed in perfect taste. The kneeling-cushions had covers of tartan silk, and a few iris had been arranged on the *tokonoma*, the alcove which is the focus of a Japanese room.

Enter the Madam, a hard-faced elderly female, but as restrained and unobtrusive as all her surroundings; then the brothel-keeper, very respectable in a brown kimono, who bowed lengthily from the threshold to his embarrassed visitors. We wanted refreshment? . . . We temporized with beer. He took his seat and made friendly conversation—not brutal-looking, more like a substantial business man, small-eyed and somewhat puffy in the jowl.

Six foreigners continued to squat about the room, and an album of the usual photographs was produced. Again we turned doubtfully from face to face, and again we had some difficulty in making a selection. Japanese prostitutes are usually peasants' daughters, mortgaged by their families when times are hard. Peasants they remain in their splendid trappings, stupid country girls with coarse hands and clumsy figures.

But we must choose. We chose and, after an interval, two girls came gliding along the passage. They bowed and crept away into different corners, where they squatted quite motionless and without expression. Neither was pretty; one was very plain, but her companion, though her teeth were stopped with gold and her skin, under the white, was pitted and ravaged, seen sideways had a trace of formal elegance, as she stooped forward, her hands upon her knees.

The Japanese coiffure, with its lustrous seashell loops, lends to the neck and shoulders of those who wear it a fragile charm which speaks unutterable submission, particularly eloquent in the long curve of the whitened nape. It is so heavy; each hair is gummed and fixed; the entire body seems to droop beneath its load. A wide sash, tightly swathed around the torso, gives the uniform convex smoothness of a thick pedestal.

Both *joro* had crudely whitened faces, the upper lip being completely whitened out. One dab of rouge on the lower lip relieved a pallor of which the intensity was almost livid. Their dresses, insipid pinks and blues, were as bright and innocent as their faces were raddled and worn. And they sat, submissively drooping with downcast eyes, and smoked the cigarettes which we had offered them in tiny puffs.

Meanwhile the proprietor explained the terms of his establishment. First the visitor's book—we must inscribe our names and addresses, our professions and other details which the police require. Now the fees—they began with a considerable cover-charge which entitled us to look but not to touch. There would be a further charge . . . after that a further charge. . . . Multiple payments are the rule on such occasions, fixed by custom and rigidly exacted by politeness; at the brothel, as at the old-fashioned Japanese inn, the mere handing over of cash becomes a ceremony.

Thus at the *machiai*, the smarter *maisons de rendezvous*, you pay a cover-charge, then 'incense-money' to the girl in accordance with the time you have kept her busy, as it is recorded by a smouldering incense-stick. . . . To-day we need not do more than pay the cover-charge, for economy had nothing to fear from inclination.

Still the talk and desultory parleying went on; and I remembered, with my back against the wall, scenes of the same kind in other countries—a tea-house, for example, in Shanghai, to which we had been taken one evening by a Chinese guide, a stout ruffianly man scarred with small-pox. It was a huge room, looking out onto a busy street, full of women sitting round little tables; to every three or four girls an ancient governess, like a peasant-woman who has brought pigeons to sell at a fair. . . . By comparison, what a refreshing informality! The young women, girls of fifteen and sixteen, wore trousers and short pyjama coats, dull blue, over white socks and little satin slippers. None was attractive, but the indistinguishable mass chattered as glib and bold as a crowd of schoolchildren. They pulled and stroked our clothes as we went by, unafraid and unabashed, almost indifferent.

No taint there of this agonizing propriety. Flesh was flesh, sold and bought—bought and enjoyed. The effect might be sinister but it was also friendly; the very cynicism of the whole proceeding sweetened the air. . . . Still, squatting immobile on their cushions, the *joro* continued to regard their knees, occasionally venturing a timid giggle at our expense. Both looked ill; the Yoshiwara has its hospital, but customers are miscellaneous and the work hard. Even now, one of them rose and slipped away, probably to spend a few minutes with some habitué who could not afford the pleasures of a protracted interview.

Her companion, the less uncomely of the pair, sat waiting, mutely waiting, at our disposal. She had a long face; her nose was slightly aquiline; her eyes, a lack-lustre oily brown, seemed as dead as the dry texture of her whitened skin. Was she glad of the brief rest, or perhaps piqued? If one assumed that she experienced either emotion, no doubt one would be exaggerating her mental suppleness. The *joro* is doubly a slave, free in law to quit the brothel when she chooses, in point of fact, since the police support the brothel-keepers, bound hand and foot to her master's service, pledged by her relations for a lump sum as irremediably as any object at a pawnshop. . . . Terrible stories are told of how, during the great earthquake, the brothel-keepers locked in the screaming girls, till the fire came and they were suffocated or burnt. They will tell you that not a single girl got clear. Things have changed. Things are always changing—on the surface. . . .

What does not change—and, in the end, proves more revelatory than hearsay, second-hand knowledge and special argument—is an attitude, a gesture you surprise, soon forgotten but which comes back with added vividness. The immemorial resignation of the painted *joro* is as remote from the bold vulgarity of the Western prostitute, as are her surroundings, with their traditional good taste, from the obstreperous gimcrack décor of a *maison de filles*. They are more harmonious, incidentally more prosaic; where prostitution is so completely unashamed, it has no need of that furtive fusty splendour which for us is the concomitant of 'gilded vice'. The brothel is the hotel on a large scale, with the amenities of 'period furnishing' into the bargain, a place of resort as respectable as any other, a voluptuous refuge from the discomforts of daily life.

Western vice pays a tribute in squalor and secrecy to the romanticism which is inseparable from the Western temperament. It was a French poet who said that the charm of love chiefly resided in the consciousness of doing wrong; and the antithesis of desire and disillusion, of physical cravings and subsequent moral nausea, has coloured some of the greatest poetry of the modern world. Even in Catullus the familiar heartbreak has begun to show, while the splendid productions of the Elizabethan drama are haunted by this perpetual harrowing conflict, between the love of life and the fear of lust, that breaks out in a thousand brilliant images:

'Talk to me somewhat quickly
Or my imagination will carry me
To see her in the shameful act of sin . . .'

cries Ferdinand when he hears of his sister's pregnancy. It is this fascinated horror of the act itself, apart from any treachery it entails, that might be expected to mystify a Japanese audience; and it is the placid reasonableness with which the Japanese envisage sex—used, at any rate, to envisage it till not long ago—that reserves so many surprises for a Western onlooker, brought up in the heady atmosphere of the Romantic poets.

The real abuses of the Yoshiwara system are the abuses of sweated labour in every country, the exploitation of the helpless by the commercially minded. . . . During the last months we spent at Tokyo, there appeared a roving group of European delegates, to investigate the traffic in women and children. Promptly—for national credit was involved —reports found their way into the English papers of girls having escaped from the Yoshiwara unhindered by the brothel-keepers or the police. After this flattering sop to their assumed principles, the Delegation was bowed quietly off the stage. Public self-esteem, faintly ruffled by their appearance, reassumed its impenetrable calm. . . .

Calm—oh, how calm, those smiling faces! 'It must be something to do with Buddhism,' the tourists say. 'The ultimate peace of Nirvana, don't you know?' . . . Immobile and utterly patient, the *joro* sat there; the proprietor was a perfect man of the world, with a pleasant touch of other-world simplicity, easy, polite, anxious to oblige. We sat round, our backs against the wall, our legs awkwardly projecting at stiff angles, drinking beer as we slaked that lust of the eye so characteristic of modern Europe and modern America. The Western races have this extraordinary passion for *seeing*—not the 'sights' merely; the Japanese are great sightseers—but the hidden aspects, the inside, of a foreign country, its brothels and its pilgrimages and its private cults, which they will presently tumble out into conversation, till deep embarrassment wreathes smiles on the Japanese countenance.

Well, we had seen. We had paid, too. And, stiff and exhausted, we staggered to our feet and took our leave. On the threshold, a row of red plush slippers, each stamped with the distinctive crest of the house, awaited us like a row of anchored sampans. Down the passage. . . . But, through the open door of a room, a last glimpse rewarded our uncomfortable session, the only object yet to come our way that so much as hinted at the real nature of the establishment. It was a coloured screen, an accomplished piece of pornography, both explicit and extremely lyrical at the same time. A young woman, as she reposed at an open window, was receiving the brisk attentions of her samurai gallant. Her chin pillowed dreamily upon her hand, she appeared to contemplate the earliest cuckoo or the falling plum-blossoms.

81

CHAPTER VIII

THE PROFESSOR AND A PICNIC

As a people, who not infrequently make it their business that their right hand should ignore what their left hand does, the Japanese find a peculiar source of strength in the landscape, the seasons, moon and flowers. Progressive—yet a philosopher at heart, hustling —yet a child of the spiritual East—this is the note which every Japanese likes to sound. Do not forget, amid modern preoccupations, the other-worldly refinement of their true characters!

Thus the Professor. There was a great deal he wanted to say, and there was still more he preferred to leave unsaid. His remarks were skilfully embroidered round large omissions; and, if what he said was beside the point, if he seldom subjected the issue to a frontal attack, his long silences had a quality all their own, vibrant and unnerving in moments of crisis.

Such a crisis had occurred when we first arrived. We were the crisis, and through the open door of the ship's saloon we watched him eye our problematic figures before darting in to effect an introduction. We shook hands; a deep silence immediately fell and, during the two days which we spent under his guardianship, long pauses and sudden fits of random small-talk alternated like bursts of gloom and sunshine on a journey through a succession of railway tunnels, the tunnels being longer than the lucid interspaces. . . .

Day and night; we had been hustled off the ship and were presently in the back seats of a car, rushing down a straight arterial road which links the twin cities of Osaka and Kobe. Osaka seemed a huge untidy place, and in the station a multitude of wooden clogs clattered deafening on acres of concrete pavement. Then Nara—with eyes that travel had dimmed we saw the park, the ancient trees, the sacred deer. We climbed up to a vermilion Shinto temple and visited the Great Buddha in his shrine, fifty feet of him rising shadowy towards the roof.

The real charm of this gigantic and hideous statue, as I ventured hopefully to point out to our companion, is dependant on the heavy coating of white dust which has drifted across its horizontal planes, dead white against a background of dim bronze, so that it has the look of a photographic negative in which the shadows show pale and the high-lights dark. 'Don't you think? . . .' I began the conversation; but the Professor allowed it to drop with a muffled thud, though he bought a picture postcard at the gate. Our equipage plunged decisively into a new tunnel, and next day when we were approaching Fujiyama it was my capacity for displaying interest which had slipped to zero. The mountain kept us company a whole hour, exquisite, unclouded from base to summit. It swept skywards through the finest of phantom curves—a little tedious in its consummate regularity.

At last Tokyo. Here the Professor broke down. Few

ordeals are so trying to a Japanese as the unrelieved companionship of a pair of foreigners, who must perpetually be talking and asking questions in their queer oddly-pitched Western voices, always attacking the right subjects in the wrong way. Or the wrong subjects. . . . This, too, is a constant peril; and our cicerone, when indicating a group of geisha who were seeing off some jovial business men on Osaka platform, had remarked acidly that Japan —the *real* Japan—was not 'like that' whatever foreigners might assume—or might declare, in the unpleasant books they often produced.

Now he collapsed. He bade us good-bye in a husky whisper and left us at the large hotel I have already described. Thence we graduated after a week of expensive comfort to matted rooms on the upper floor of a Japanese inn. . . . The Professor, meanwhile, had learned his lesson; but there is no gainsaying the Japanese sense of duty. He invited us to a picnic he had arranged—'a little party to celebrate your coming'.

Our picnic was not held in the open country, which would have been difficult or almost impossible to find within a twenty mile radius of the sprawling capital, but in a tea-garden conveniently placed in a neighbouring suburb, to which a file of taxis conducted us at noon. The Professor rather tensely led the way, followed by his wife and daughters carrying baskets. Himself he carried a bulky German camera, and seldom addressed his family except to issue a brief command.

A mild and sunny afternoon it happened to be. We passed a gate and were presently wandering up an alley, among the shrubs, rocks and gazebos of a deserted pleasure ground. At this time of year there were few visitors, and at the lake's edge a dozen painted skiffs, with prows in the form of swans or dragons, were huddled together under the charge of an old man. It was all a little melancholy and yet appealing; the empty boats, a tufted island on the water, and the slow carp which swam languidly amid the lily-roots, but came to the surface with a great threshing when food was thrown—big spongy cakes pulled from a long thread. . . .

Then they arrowed up and in a moment the dark water was alive with stout patriarchal fish, white—a leprous white—or golden red, silken grey, fish oddly streaked and spotted, thrusting forward gill to gill around the cakes, sucking them down and smothering and swamping them in blind greed, while the onlookers laughed and stamped on the wooden jetty. A deep guzzling sound accompanied the fishes' meal, and later, when the food had been exhausted and their stout shapes had glided off to the muddy bottom, a massive carp would momentarily reappear and, lifting its large mouth free of the water—a black hole bored in the smooth surface—would engulf with succulent emphasis a floating crumb, then turn and glisten sideways out of view.

Feeding the carp was but one of many diversions. For example, there was the potter who kept a stand where he fired the unbaked vessels his customers painted, after dipping them into a clear and sticky glaze. Every Japanese is fond of the word 'souvenir' and it was noticeable that, although his foreign guests embarked on a variety of designs, niggling, fanciful and uncommemorative, the Professor took a large beaker and a clean brush, and devoted his skill to creating a memento of the afternoon, on which he asked us, when he had finished, to paint our names, observing that it would be a valuable record.

The picnic lasted until the evening, and we ate two solid meals during its course. The typical inclemency of a Western picnic, consumed out of doors upon the ground, exposed to the freaks of wind and sunshine, had been circumvented by the hire of a small pavilion, with its own paper shutters and separate privy. This summer-house was in the neighbourhood of the waterfall, and the cascade, a great attraction of the place, dashed in a feathery jet over the rocks and plunged sheer into a shallow pebble basin, thence rippling among boulders down a stream-bed which was overlooked by the starry foliage of young maples.

Several adjacent pavilions were grouped about, arranged as carefully as the arbours and summer-houses in a Chinese landscape, with the same effect of slightly specious picturesqueness. Ours, I remember, stood the highest, so that we commanded another cottage across the stream, in which two men and a woman were passing the day, the men extended comfortably upon the mats, while the woman, beneath her helmet of glossy hair, leant forward in a slack curve from neck to waist, smiling down with quiet intimacy at her companions, whose cheerful voices were lost in the rush of water. . . . I remember thinking that, if I stayed in Tokyo, I would write a story around this strange suburban pleasance, half shabby and half rural, among the tramlines, with its dusty rocks and sinuous sanded paths and its waterfall which could be turned on and off at will.

Yes, the waterfall would have delighted Bishop Berkeley; it only existed as long as it was perceived. Should one transfer one's admiration and walk away, a coolie, high up at its unseen source, turned off the brilliant foaming thread and through the silence which descended mysteriously over the garden one caught the distant grating of a tram or the faint toot of a motor-horn behind the boskage.

Here was the setting, but no story ever materialized. It must be commonplace and yet memorable, like the scene; lovers, a young foreigner and his Japanese mistress—a geisha, I supposed, from a smart tea-house—who met behind the privacy of paper walls, in the off-season when the garden was almost deserted. A geisha—since a 'respectable' Japanese woman would be difficult to situate properly in such a romance. Neither the Professor's wife nor his eldest daughter seemed constructed for any existence but that of work—hard work, marriage and frequent child-bearing—as they tugged at the heavy baskets and laid the plates, whispering in hushed tones among themselves and shrinking back when we sat down to begin our picnic.

'They do not speak English,' the Professor had said. That settled it; and they crouched dumbly upon their heels, observing us with the liquid gaze of patient kine or sliding forward to deposit a rasher of red beef in the pan which was hissing over the charcoal and from which we served ourselves by the help of awkward chopsticks. They were contented; their turn would soon come; and the Master of the House, whose squatting shape expressed dignity, *savoir-faire* and determination, threw them over his shoulder a reflected glory, for there could be no doubt that his picnic was going well.

Once—only once—was there a hitch. It was not serious but it evoked from the Professor a sharp reproof to his family in general. 'I am telling them that they do not know how to wait!' he observed for our benefit when he had finished. 'Oh, but Professor . . .' objected tremulously his foreign friends. 'Everything is splendid! . . .' And, after a brief embarrassed pause, we again took up our chopsticks and crammed our mouths with the insouciance of hardened tourists in a Latin country.

A tourist exaggerates the sufferings of domesitic animals—it is a reflection from which we have most of us obtained comfort. 'Of course,' we agreed privately, 'they didn't mind,' and: 'You know, dear,' said the already experienced lady whose knowledge of the life was more extensive, 'Japanese women are brought up to act as servants. So what may seem a little hard to us. . . .' We nodded; East was East, after all, and one must beware of the vacuous generalizations which are the plague of those who indulge in writing books. . . . No sooner had we finished our own meal and risen to stretch our legs and take the air, than our attendants made a circle where we had left them and the 'second service' as in a restaurant car got under way.

It was not long before they joined us near the stream, now acting as escort and devoted nursemaids to a pair of little boys in sailor suits, chubby and dark-faced, who wanted to paddle. 'You can fish,' said the Professor to his company. Gardeners, in straw hats and blue coolie-coats, appeared, each carrying a wooden bucket which he emptied into the water of a secluded pool, sowing its golden shallows with flickering movement as the tiny two-tailed scarlet fish escaped like threads of fire among the rocks. Human beings followed, shouting and splashing, wetting one another while they grabbed. Perversely, I felt sorry for the fish. On the whole, though, it was an edifying spectacle, placid, good-humoured and domestic, gay but never rowdy and unrestrained. Japanese have an inimitable faculty of enjoying themselves within the margins of decorum, of being cheerful and yet subdued at the same time. The sweaty tumult of Hampstead Heath on a Bank Holiday, the squalling children, jaded mothers and cross men, would be abhorrent to the Japanese sense of values. A crowd, which is at liberty, behaves well; even the rolling red-cheeked drunks are not obtrusive.

A holiday is a ceremonial occasion, and as such is not only to be enjoyed but must be commemorated by some small but appropriate purchase. Snapshots and group photographs are almost obligatory; and the Professor's beautiful expensive German camera was soon levelled at the scene from every angle and clicked off with a certain ceremonious sharpness, as he perched on the hummock of a smooth stone. For the moment I believe he was really happy; he had laid aside, though it was not for very long, the awful weight of his professorial responsibilities, with results which were both endearing and somehow pathetic. A short figure becoming baggy about the paunch—I used to liken him, in a less amicable mood, to a middle-aged ruminative Belgian hare, the rodent's eyes and the rodent's solemn face and a feeling that he would nip your finger from sheer nervousness.

He did his duty; he was dutiful to the very marrow, and I dare say that, if he had anticipated his own epitaph, few appreciations would have flattered him more profoundly. He was the Bureaucrat—the Japanese bureaucrat—par excellence, in a land where the orders of petty officialdom are as numerous as in Germany before the War, and where uniforms command as much respect; any uniform—

though obscure and badly paid, the man who carries it mirrors on every button some glint of the supreme imperial dignity that forms the invisible apex of the social pyramid. The policeman, in his box along the lane, supports his functions with the haughty consequence of a Cabinet Minister. Ordinary citizens doff their caps when asking the way; he answers them indifferently, *de haut en bas*. He is Authority, and there can be no deeper satisfaction where the fountain-head of all authority is semi-divine.

It was as a seraph in the immense hierarchy of official paradise that the Professor had introduced us to this queer Eden. But now the summer day was beginning to go down; the moist twilight, which had crept out from under the trees, brought with it all those faint and cloying odours, the scent of evergreens, the smell of vegetables and fish, that give the Japanese dusk its peculiar airless quality, so that it resembles the vitreous gloom of some great hothouse. . . . The women had packed the baskets and tidied the children; we set forth in single file towards the gate. As we receded, the loud whisper of the romantic waterfall was suddenly quenched and we heard the noises of the city.

PART II
TOKYO

CHAPTER I

THE UNIVERSITY

From my account of our first arrival at Tokyo I have omitted one intimidating circumstance. The locomotive snorted wearily to rest and, tired out after a long journey and much sightseeing, we stumbled from the high step of the pullman carriage and found ourselves . . . There drawn up in a neat crescent, uniformed, spectacled, all eyes, was a large deputation of young men. Brass buttons, brass badges on peaked caps which were removed with a simultaneous flourish; a spokesman moved forward from the ranks and tendered a gilt basket full of flowers—flesh-pink gladiolæ if I remember right—while pronouncing some tremendous phrase of welcome; at which the solid phalanx in the rear bowed deeply like corn before the wind.

A year passed, fourteen months to be precise; and once more we were on the platform of Tokyo station. This time the scene was less imposing. The crowd was smaller, a mere group of twenty or thirty, gathered to bid us good-bye as we left Japan. There was no longer the same attitude of tense expectancy; a few friends were sorry to see us go, and the Professor rose dutifully to the occasion and waved his straw hat after the train. We stood and waved as the platform glided off, a brightly lit steel-girdered concrete shed, populous with bowing and smiling marionettes. . . . We went into the restaurant car and ordered whisky—glad and a little mournful at our escape.

Glad to be leaving Tokyo and Japan; mournful because a year, however unpleasant, is a year which one can ill afford to lose. Mournful, too, because the company on the platform seemed to reproach me with my precipitate retreat. It was not that I should be regretted for myself; I symbolized another failure to establish contact. . . . I had come; I had certainly not vanquished. I had seen and been seen and gone away. Foreign professors are many and they change often; but, as they step inside the magic circle of Japanese life, a hundred eyes, hopeful and inquisitive, search them for some 'message' they cannot produce. Immense respect, deep attention, yearning silence—then disenchantment, devastating and profound. The lifted gaze of the students in the classroom drops suddenly towards the inevitable feet of clay.

Personally, I felt happier and more at ease, once my all too-human pedestal had been laid bare. The first weeks were both arduous and bewildering. Enquiries as to my 'impressions' of the country—could I say that I was astonished by the number of telegraph poles?—alternated with the politely expressed hope that I should live to become a 'second Lafcadio Hearn' and rear a large family in their midst. I had no intention, if I could help it, of doing either, and, perhaps, did not dissimulate with sufficient thoroughness. Incidentally, I soon learned that the Japanese are, as a race, heroically insensitive to boredom.

Thus, a tea party, lasting four to five hours, at which twenty to thirty speeches were delivered in painstaking but slow and broken English, was for them a perfectly normal entertainment which did not demand a special display of fortitude. It was held under cover of a draughty drillhall; and sugared cakes and ham sandwiches and slices of beef were washed down with a thin and sweetish beverage which resembled the cold dregs of watery cocoa. And then the speeches—they were as flattering as they were long. Student after student, grasping his notes, rose from his seat at the trestle table and began to walk the vertiginous tightrope of English eloquence. Some quoted Tennyson in mid-career; some read aloud to me my own verses. And all, whether self-assured or timid, indicated the splendid future which stretched before us.

Many referred proudly to 'our alma mater'. Here, at least, my impressions had been distinct. The University was attached to a big school, and its buildings—they were not yet ready for occupation—were packed away behind the roofs of the school proper, a vague group of two-storeyed wooden sheds scattered about a huge and dusty playground. Little to please a casual foreign eye; the sheds themselves were slatternly and needed painting, while the main path which led to the University was almost impassable with deep mire when the rain fell.

Mud and dust and dirty noisesome corridors; memories of the dismal period spent at school were wafted back with the stench of acid from a laboratory and the stifling fog of chalk-dust in the classrooms. Good-bye to any fantasies I had entertained of the lecture hall, with its slightly Buddhist atmosphere, in which I discoursed to squatting rows of silk-clad acolytes. Desks and an overheated iron stove, fusty uniforms which suggested a congress of youthful tram conductors. . . .

Nor were they particularly youthful if it came to that. The tunics and brass buttons which they wore gave them a look of decorous juvenility, but with very few exceptions they were all married and most the devoted fathers of several children. For the moment they only existed in the mass, deadly quiet, utterly earnest as I entered the room, fountain pens poised above their notebooks, ready to catch each word that left my lips. Such responsiveness was unnerving after a while; it was uncanny, the tense absorption of their attitude; and not until the end of my opening lecture did they inform me that they had scarcely retained a syllable. My voice, they pointed out, was very odd, my delivery a mere Niagara of foreign sounds. With all the indirectness at their command, they hinted that it might be well if I tried dictation.

Lafcadio Hearn dictated every lecture—every sentence and the punctuation too. I gave in, and the industrious fountain pens were soon squeaking competitively beneath my desk. *John Webster*—1575 *to* 1624—*the dates of his birth and death are equally doubtful. After Shakespeare, the author of 'The Duchess of Malfi' is one of the best-known Elizabethan dramatists.* . . . Not the finest method of imparting a knowledge of English literature, but a method which apparently suits the Japanese. A student may not understand what you are saying, but he takes it down and, in the process of taking it down, feels that he has made a tangible acquisition. A page of notes is so wonderfully definite; it is knowledge. A mystic reverence for the written word lends it a value quite independent of its meaning. So long as the pen-nib is kept busy, the lecturer and his audience are both at peace.

Few professions are more cynical than pedagogy, and I seemed to recognize in my own behaviour towards my pupils the dejected droop of a dozen forgotten school-masters. Even our mannerisms were painfully alike— brisk entry, growing lassitude and hurried departure; as they had done in the interval between the periods, I wandered off to the dusty recesses of the senior common-room. It contained among other objects a large ping-pong table; and here, with much excitement, in their shirt sleeves, two of the younger masters were usually buffeting the tiny ball. At his desk, a little apart from his subordinates, the Professor swept up the crumbs of a picnic lunch; while my friend Z, the most cultivated of the faculty, sat puzzling over an annotated Dryden.

'Interesting poem *Annus Mirabilis*' he would observe.

'I'm sure it is. I've never read it,' I had to confess. The ancient janitor, who was diligent in brewing tea and, as far as I could ascertain, did nothing more, now arrived with two insipid pale green cupfuls which he handed, bowing deeply, on a small tray.

'I am giving the second-year students some readings from Waller. "*Go lovely rose. . . .*"—I am very fond of it. . . .'

'Do they know much about Waller?' I would enquire.

'Not at present. But they are very anxious to learn. You must remember. . . .'

But at this stage we were frequently interrupted by a cautious hiss and scuffle from the background, and Mr. X, embracing a volume of the *Oxford Dictionary*, would glide in to ask the derivation of a phrase:

'Just a moment, please! The expression "top-notch" . . . We are studying O. Henry next period, and I cannot quite get the hang of the following sentence. There! That is colloquial, I imagine? . . . "Top-notch" and "top-hole", are they the same?'

Mr. X had an ogreish appetite for information, and his big face and broadly flashing teeth glistened in a naive ecstasy of self-improvement. The queries he put were mainly philological, and I preferred them to the more literary type of question:

'Excuse me,' would begin a colleague I hardly knew, stopping me in the quadrangle on my way home, 'but what is your opinion of Thomas Hardy? Can I describe him as a metaphysical writer?'

'It depends, I suppose, on what you mean by metaphysical.'

'Andrew Lang says, I think, in one of his essays that Hardy is a philosophical realist.'

'Then I should take his word for it, Mr. W.'

'Many thanks, sir.' And the questioner would back away, leaving the impression that he was slightly disappointed. Somehow I had failed to recognize my cue; a certain flippancy marred the oracle's replies. Could it be that, after coming all this distance, I had no conception of English literature as a school-subject?

And what was it I was reported to have said the other day?—that it was more valuable to enjoy a bad book than to trudge conscientiously through a good one, that enjoyment was the only justification of reading! Such rumours travel fast in the Japanese world, telegraphed with mysterious efficiency from person to person, gradually encompassing the individual they concern till he is aware of a faint vibration all around him. It is like an adult game of Hunt the Slipper; accost any member of the circle and he reveals a smiling face and empty hands. But the ubiquitous slipper travels on, accompanied by a low rustle of excitement.

Add to this, that a subsidized university is directly controlled by the Department of Education—hence bureaucratic both in its methods and in its outlook—and the atmosphere of the senior common-room as I learned to know it may become a little more vivid to the English mind. Modern Japan is a paradise of bureaucrats; every lecturer at a government school or university thinks of himself primarily as an official, and to succeed, must have the official point of view. Politically and socially, he must be irreproachable, a prolific father, a staunch patriot, a good conservative. He must win the guarded respect of his jealous colleagues, without incurring their animosity by undue brilliance. He must be *sound*—as sound as the Professor, sound as a solid undistinguished bell which returns the right note wherever you touch it; for the Professor, in his virtues and his shortcomings, was fairly representative of the type.

I revert to the Professor with alacrity; he fascinates me now as he did then. Was he the Metternich I sometimes thought? His policy of majestic *laisser-faire* was too thorough-going to be anything but deliberate; yet, on the other hand, my observations of his private character seemed to show him as a simple kindly soul. Was he merely capitalizing his own deficiencies? 'The Professor', explained a friend who knew him well, 'is a sort of policeman; you must never forget that. He has read English literature and learned his subject, as a policeman learns the contents of his little book.' Exactly! and as a policeman might make it his business to keep out of harm's way in serious trouble so the Professor, when difficulties arose, was miraculously but inevitably 'not there'.

He vanished; I had difficulty about text books, difficulty about the curriculum and methods of work. One flustered subordinate sweated and giggled, while the Professor lurked omnisciently behind the scenes. This characteristic strategem, I was afterwards told, he did not confine to his management of difficult foreigners; it had been noticed by his students and Japanese colleagues, who passed it round among themselves with acid commentary. Even the Professor was a target for public criticism; Japanese society is ruled from below as well as from above. No less powerful than the dread of immediate superiors is the dread of sharp-tongued colleagues and tattling subordinates.

Thus the constitution of a Japanese university, autocratic when judged by Western standards, has also a very democratic side. That the faculty were afraid of one another was sufficiently obvious in everything they did; more remarkable—it had not occurred to me all at once—they were as nervously upon tiptoe with their own students. At first sight the students were hardly formidable; but, like a diver who having reached the ocean floor learns to accustom his eyes to strange conditions, I soon learned to pick out in my new existence shades and subtleties of terrifying import. Almost morbidly well-disciplined the students appeared; their respectful attitude towards their teachers was much advertised. I now discovered that this traditional respect was concentrated not on the man but on the idea—on the Teacher as he is laid up in Platonic heaven, by no means on his fallible human deputy. The measure of their regard for the Perfect Teacher might be calculated by their ruthlessness towards his substitutes.

To describe the persistent pressure from below, 'ruthless' is no doubt too strong a word. Yet the influence of the assembled students is a fact; they change the curriculum and hold meetings when they please, very often cutting short a lecture to do so. At the more chaotic private universities they break out in extremely effective strikes. Elsewhere their opposition is seldom explicit; but alas for the lecturer whom they oppose! They come late; they forget to bring their books; they sit with folded arms and glumly gaze upon him. He asks questions and his questions go unanswered. They crush him beneath a dead weight of obstinate mutism. . . .

So much for a disaffected class. Students in a more equable frame of mind positively sparkle with the willingness to please. No commission is too onerous if they can help you; their good humour is as exacting as their discontent. They are charming then, yet rarely individual. Always between the lecturer and his students hangs a curtain that may grow slighter but never dissolves. He knows nothing of their real tastes and private preferences; he continues to know nothing until the end. They put forth cautious tentacles from time to time, withdraw them hurriedly and shrink away into the mass.

Public opinion dominates the mass, and no student wishes to stand out. Little trace here of that irritable egotism which is characteristic of the English undergraduate; uniformity, not singularity, is their aim, and a student when he speaks to you before the others is careful simply to voice the general view: '*We* think—*We* have been taught'—is his refrain. The first person singular is not at a premium. Admirable, but in the long run how stupefying! I have spent hours trying to squeeze from my Japanese friends some authentic and highly-coloured personal prejudice. With a skill I could not but admire they eluded me and took refuge in generalities.

Sometimes I would bait my hook with a confession, and by admitting a preference try to attract theirs. . . . Bland incredulity was the only result or, should I refer to a visit I had made, some hackneyed and standardized piece of information which might have come from a guide-book or a school essay: 'We call that one of the seven beautiful views. . . . Do you mean to climb Fuji in the autumn? The Professor took a party up last year.' An English undergraduate would have detested Fuji and told me as much with caustic satisfaction. Conversely, he might have been interested in rock-climbing and recommended another mountain further away.

No scintilla of that kind could I ever strike. It was not that I found my students exactly colourless, though in the mass it was hard to distinguish them clearly; they resembled a murky and faded portrait group, which one must rub if separate figures are to emerge. A thick varnish covered the whole canvas; and, while here and there, it seems to me as I look back, I managed to distinguish a definite outline, the chiaroscuro of an unmistakable personality, on the whole this shadowy composition remained as dim and self-subdued as I had originally found it.

One or two distinct figures, and that is all; the oldest member, the spokesman of the group, possessed by a stern sense of duty, honest, bespectacled, rather severe, a little ponderous in his relations with myself—I appreciate but am somewhat awed by sterling qualities—and yet kind; for on the day I left Japan he presented me with a beautifully written manuscript, the fair copy of an essay I had praised, thirty pages without a blot or a misspelling, 'in memory of his hearing my eminent lectures'. I wonder if he will succeed in Japanese life. I hope so, and I am sure that the 'star pupil' will continue his triumphant upward march, cautious and soft-voiced, for many years. Incidentally, he was very good-looking, somewhat masklike that elegantly designed face with the straight nose, high forehead and broad cheekbones; much neater in his appearance than any of the others, even dandified; he hissed slightly when he spoke and had accomplished—almost too accomplished—manners. Every virtue, I feel confident, was his—every talent, except the germ of originality.

Two portraits; I will add a third and fourth; the sharp-nosed perpetually smiling lover of nature who was hard at work translating Richard Jeffries. Very turgid, those grimly pastoral pages; but the translator, though often at a loss, never flagged in his admiration for the English essayist. Lambs and catkins are wholly absent from the Japanese scene; but, although many of the objects he found described were as unfamiliar to him as the landscape of the moon, somehow he derived pleasure from what he read. A much worldlier personage comes next; when I left him he was struggling up to the eyes in the splendid but tortured lyricism of John Donne; plump-faced, amiable, a trifle malicious, he spoke in the full-throated burring tone best described by the adjective *grasseyant*. The wildly elusive genius of the English poet he followed up with half-humorous pertinacity. 'Very interesting—*very* difficult . . .' he would murmur, smiling dazedly and rumpling his locks.

Here, then, were some figures in the group; and it is pleasant to add that their kindness during our stay was of a quality I do not expect to meet again. When good-tempered, the selflessness of the Japanese, their willingness to take trouble on one's behalf, is only less notable than their intransigeance when annoyed. Selfless! But one is interested in the Self and in other people's selves as much as one's own. The Self—that was the quarry which eluded me; personal judgments, original criticism, startling flashes, which are the charm and the perplexity of the Western world. There was no escape from these stereotyped opinions which, even though they were a blind and nothing more, slipped down with the solidity of a steel shutter. The very students who seemed at first sight most receptive showed the same tenacity in keeping their distance.

For a brief moment their true opinions sometimes appeared. I remember asking if a married Japanese friend had any children. 'His wife is barren,' said a student; and the point of view came with disconcerting clarity. She was sterile; there could be no other explanation, and the childless wife was registered in his mind as a catastrophic freak, like a barren cow. A chance remark, yet it goes far towards illuminating the unscrupulousness of Japanese foreign policy. . . .

And what of their feeling for the English language? Some, I am afraid, following the Professor, regarded it as an indispensable adjunct and read Shelley with the enthusiasm of young careerists. To others it meant a confused aspiration, all the more intense for being vague. In both instances its value was symbolic; it represented either a step on the road to prosperity or a roosting-place for every type of improbable idealism. And neither party was content to read literature by the light of purely literary standards. No, 'high thoughts' must immediately be invoked; and it was extraordinary what a profusion of noble sentiments, 'lessons' and 'messages' and similar bric-a-brac, they could unearth if called on to produce an essay. One of the first English books translated into Japanese was the celebrated *Self Help* of Samuel Smiles. It enjoyed an immense success when it appeared, and its baneful effect can still be felt to-day.

Life is a battle, remarks the student in his essay, and hints at some portentous wrestling match waged between himself and the forces of circumstance. One is inclined to shrug one's shoulders and read on; but perhaps, after the twentieth reiteration—all students essays are strangely similar—one begins to see the cliché in a new aspect. Though banal, it has some reference to the truth. Few lives are less enviable at the present time than that of the average Japanese student, over-educated and not infrequently underfed, ambitious, idealistic and usually poor, obliged to face a series of examinations, often in a peculiarly difficult foreign tongue, but with little prospect, should he pass them, of getting work. Suicide and tuberculosis are equally common; it was Lafcadio Hearn, I believe, who pointed out the hardship of requiring adolescents, brought up on a diet of rice and fish, to digest the culture of the meat-eating Western races. Breakdowns are reported year by year; and in an old tree in the gardens of a university—not the university to which I was originally attached, but another and more venerable institution—I was shown the crooked bough over a lily pond from which a student had hanged himself not long ago.

Education is a Moloch in Japan, worshipped with the sacrifice of life and health, to the accompaniment of Victorian copy-book maxims. 'Knowledge is power' intones its priest; but knowledge, granted the conditions of the modern world, is very often a disability rather than an advantage. To prepare oneself for the life of a village schoolmaster, or for work in an office or a bank, by the intensive study of nineteenth-century English literature is neither economic nor desirable. Schools and universities cover Japan, methodically turning out into the world young men whom its machinery cannot absorb. In theory they are qualified modern citizens, in practice unemployable and unemployed. . . .

Still the scramble for education goes on. A young man, who had seen my photograph in a Tokyo newspaper, appeared one morning clad in a tail-coat, a white slip, striped trousers and varnished shoes—palpably hired out by the day—announcing that he wished to become my servant, unsalaried, for the mere privilege of learning English. An assistant wrote a letter from a shop, offering friendship and proposing a few questions: 'Pardon me, but I write to you the private letter. Why came you to Japan? Or who? . . . I am graduated from commercial school a year ago. I think to learn more and more study English while in school. Therefore I wish to make an acquaintance with a foreigner—always.' An engaging approach; but how could it be met? Even had the writer obtained his wish and acquired a considerable proficiency in the English language, his opportunities of practising it would be very scarce. A typical and pathetic victim of the current mania, he must be left alone to fulfil his dubious destiny.

Modernity, 'up-to-dateness'—that is the rage, a passion not of yesterday nor of to-day, but as old almost, it would seem, as the Japanese people. Thus the courtiers of the remote Heian period, during the ninth century of our era, imitated Chinese verse and Chinese fashions, brought over from the cosmopolitan T'ang capital, and used 'old-fashioned' as the supreme term of contempt. Later, it was the turn of Western traders, and young elegants of the sea-ports in which they lived went so far as to adopt Western modes. They wore baggy breeches and smoked tobacco; while Christianity was 'taken up' by rich and poor. Another long period of seclusion; then the Meiji, the birth of modern Japan. German architects, English schoolmasters and American missionaries made hay beneath the sunshine of the enlightened epoch. . . .

The metamorphosis was devastating but incomplete. There is some element, strongly rooted in the Japanese soul, that resists every effort at transformation. It is as though a shy and egocentric man, who yearns for the society of his fellow mortals, for the cheerful promiscuity of everyday life, should attempt with periodic and desperate violence to wrench free from his own innate reserve. He is determinedly sociable but always lonely. Sooner or later, the introspective mood returns, his spirit bends back upon itself; and so Japan, after every spasm of change, has retired once more to airless isolation.

Will it, or can it, happen again? Not as thoroughly as it has happened in the past. Japan must go forward or go down; unless she is to sink, she must keep moving. This, at least, is what the Japanese say themselves; but there are signs that the protracted farce of 'Western culture' may before long be measurably abridged. Already there is talk among the authorities of dropping English as a compulsory school subject. It is learnt in Japan as French is learnt in England, with results that are scarcely more impressive. Few Japanese can speak English at all fluently, and most of them, though they have laboured over it at school, are in command only of one or two broken sentences which they are too nervous or too conceited to employ. English retains its talismanic value, but chiefly for the unsophisticated and the pedagogic. Intellectuals are nowadays looking elsewhere; French and Russian stars are in the ascendant. And the star with ever so faintly a reddish twinkle can be sure of a large following of young astronomers.

A red star hangs westward above Moscow, and many eyes, some fascinated and some alarmed, glance up in its direction with furtive enquiry; furtive, since to be seen so much as peeping is immediately to be convicted of 'dangerous thought', and the student or the schoolboy who thinks dangerously may be expelled without a hearing by the police. These expulsions occur so often that they are barely news; schoolboys and even professors of universities—there was a recent case at the University of Kyoto—are degraded on the smallest provocation. It is not necessary to be a theoretical communist; mild socialism is dangerous enough, any criticism, however slight, of the existing order. . . . One is not surprised that the more adventurous students—in larger numbers, it is said, every year—should adhere with painful devotion to a hopeless cause, though it entails a kind of social *harakiri*.

Families are divided and friendships broken. Under the smooth surface of Japanese life, such dramas are continually being enacted; and here and there a more than usually honest friend provides a brief glimpse into the depths. 'It is like a web,' melodramatically exclaimed Z; 'those at the centre get hold of a young man; they involve him and never let him go!' By a more level-headed acquaintance I was informed that, when the Communists were anxious to gain a partisan, they took steps to have him arrested for a minor offence. They realized that, after a day or two of police detention—*habeas corpus* is skilfully 'got round' and detention is often accompanied by the third degree—he would come out as ardent a communist as they could wish. . . .

The police station is a thriving factory of young communists; and, no doubt, the general embargo on free speech—carried to the most brutal and stupid lengths against boys of sixteen and seventeen—helps considerably to accelerate production. As marked is its effect upon the orthodox; an atmosphere of slyness and mistrust, of silly suspicious carping and conscious rectitude distinguishes the personality of right-thinkers. Sternly orthodox were the students I knew best; future pedagogues and servants of the state, it would have cost them their livelihood to be anything else; yet I noticed that the mere mention of Marx's name seemed to afford them a delightfully illicit thrill. Marx to them was like Machiavelli to an Elizabethan. Sometimes they shyly tampered with the forbidden subject and enjoyed stirring up its gloomy associations.

I remember, for instance, asking a student if he could explain to me the title of a literary group, to which one of my Japanese friends belonged—a perfectly harmless group, I hasten to add, called the M.E.L. group, which stands for Modern English Literature, though at the time I had not grasped its derivation. I asked him what the three letters meant.

'Some people', he replied with grisly coyness, sinking his voice to a low sepulchral whisper, 'say they stand for Marx, Engels and Lenin. . . .' I passed on this interpretation to my friend, and in the next manifesto the group produced room was found for an indignant and flurried disclaimer. I have also heard that a lecture on *Piers Plowman* had extremely embarrassing consequences for a Japanese colleague. . . .

Yet in spite of everything, dangerous thought is rampant. There are proletarian films, subversive novels, while but a few doors from the Imperial University a bookshop has mysteriously escaped suspicion, though crammed from floor to ceiling with communist literature. And then there are the 'Marx-boys' in the street—students dressed in ancient tattered kimono, unshaven, with shocks of dishevelled hair hanging down greasily across their shoulders, so that they resemble the later Merovingian monarchs. Their slovenliness is the uniform of their convictions, and they swagger past in aggressive twos and threes, haughty and rather pathetic and much alone. A plump student, fresh from reading *The Essays of Elia*, gives them a wide berth as they go by.

CHAPTER II

DANGEROUS THOUGHT AND MODERN LITERATURE

But thought need not be dangerous to be disturbing, and many students seem to have discovered in foreign literature a safety-valve for their sense of social injustice. On one occasion, never to be forgotten, I interviewed some sixty or seventy graduates, anxious to gain a diploma in advanced English, during a protracted *viva voce* examination. What modern English writers had they read? Did they admire So-and-So? And why? The victim would breathe deeply and rub his face, give a slight gasp and launch out into the unknown:

'I admire Galsworthy, because he sees life as a struggle; he writes about injustice, about poverty. John Galsworthy is champion of the poor. . . .'

'Thank you!' *Beta minus* I would note down. 'Next please! You say that you admire Hardy. What is it you admire in Hardy's novels?'

'I admire Hardy, because he describes the life of peasants. Hardy is prophet of the lower classes.'

'Any other reason? He is very popular in Japan. Can you give a reason for his popularity?'

'I think it is because he appeals to Japanese pessimism. Japanese are a very pessimistic race. . . .'

On this last point, most candidates were agreed. Hardy's pessimism, so uncomplicated and almost placid that it suggests an old man in a muddy lane poking with his umbrella after a bad smell—probably a stillborn lamb behind the hedge—rouses a responsive echo in Japanese breasts. Subtlety of presentation they do not require, subtle shades, in nine instances out of ten, being altogether beyond their mental scope. It is not merely that the Japanese as a people have a systematic and moralizing bent, which leads them to prefer the edifying to the elusive; but one must remember the immense differences of background which hold up their appreciation at every step.

Even the landscape of English literature is utterly strange; for a poem as serenely obvious as Gray's *Elegy* makes mention in its magnificent opening lines of some half a dozen objects familiar to us, but to which Japan in its length and breadth provides no parallel. What of the church tower and its 'ivy-mantled' walls? Does a schoolboy, when he is precipitated into Gray's poem, see the Buddhist temple of the village in which he was born, with its dusky front, spreading eaves and stone-paved court; or some ugly Wesleyan chapel in a Tokyo suburb? Of the churchyard he might form a vague conception, and it is possible that for the curfew of the first line, an English bell tanging out from a cobwebbed loft, the bellropes rasping and squeaking amid the beams, while an old sexton pulls sleepily down below, he might substitute the fuller booming resonance of a Buddhist bell solemnly thudded at dawn and dark. 'Lowing herds' there may be in the northern island, but there are none in the vicinity of the large cities; the 'drowsy tinklings' of the sheep-bells in distant folds are remote from any music in his experience.

The magic of association is all gone, and what is left is the moralistic burden, which, as it happens, might be strangely sympathetic. Most students at a Japanese university are youths 'to Fortune and to Fame unknown', and many of them, at the warning touch of phthisis, brought on by under-nourishment and overwork in the crowded students' lodging-houses in which they live, may have responded to the exquisite poignancy of the English verse:

'For who, to dumb Forgetfulness a prey,
This pleasing anxious being e'er resigned,
Left the warm precincts of the cheerful day,
Nor cast one longing ling'ring look behind?'

But Gray's *Elegy* is not the whole of English verse, and *Jude* not the crowning achievement of modern fiction. Elsewhere, there are difficulties on every page. The Japanese is confronted in his reading by a psychology so different from his own that it evokes the classic concision of a famous dialogue:

' "You see a dog growls when it's angry, and wags its tail when it's pleased. Now *I* growl when I'm pleased and wag my tail when I'm angry. . . ."

' "*I* call it purring, not growling," said Alice.

' "Call it what you like," said the Cat. . . .'

Call it what you like, but there it is. The fact remains—to state the difference at its simplest—that a Japanese, very angry or deeply wretched, for example, if he has lost a close relation, produces a wan but extensive smile from ear to ear and giggles with a desperate hiccupping noise, which becomes more desperate as his grief grows more profound.

Disconcerting, but, of course, superficial. As antagon-istic is the Japanese sense of propriety which crops out at the most unexpected moments. Prudery one hardly looks for in Japan, where even the toy shops contain naively indecent toys—badgers made of coloured cotton-wool, with huge distended stomachs and enormous genitals—and where the phallic cult is widespread and unashamed. Offended prudery is not a reasonable emotion; and the Japanese ideal of subservient womanhood is often as gravely upset by Western heroines, as some missionary by a stone phallus in a Japanese rice field. Once when read-ing a story by Aldous Huxley, in which a married woman advises an anxious virgin to 'go to bed with the young man if she wants to', a student stopped me to enquire if I wasn't shocked. I had to admit that I was neither shocked nor much surprised. We looked at one another sadly, and then went on. . . .

Huxley is diligently read by the young *avant-garde*, as are Joyce, Virginia Woolf and D. H. Lawrence. It is their modernity, after all, which counts, and to satisfy this crav-ing for the new no effort is too purposeless nor too back-breaking. Imagine *Ulysses* translated into Japanese! Yet such a venture, I am told, is under way. And, at the same time, more conservative lovers of English are laboriously annotating *The Ring and the Book*. . . . Literature for its own sake is unimportant. There are exceptions; dear Z, at the University, studies Smollett and Longinus with equal pleasure, and composes Japanese renderings of Charles d'Orléans. Not only does he read: he understands. But then, Z is an exception to the rule, a little cut off from the larger number of his compatriots who are persevering or scholarly rather than brilliant.

For brilliance—the cynical brilliance of the West, the suppleness and adaptability of the Chinese—is not a common commodity in Japan. On arriving, I had pictured the Japanese as a sharp-witted, uncannily acute race, endowed by nature with every superficial gift. At a first acquaintance, the very opposite proved true; hesitating, tongue-tied and always nervous, they suggested a people of adolescents, alternately assertive and depreciatory, prone to sudden collapses and odd recoveries, to spurts of rudeness and long intervals of embarrassment, over-eager, over-calculating, over polite. In contrast to the mental image I had acquired—it is shared, I suppose, by most foreigners who speak patronizingly of the 'clever little Japs'—I noticed the extreme slowness of their mental processes and the agony it obviously cost them to come to a decision. Time—a Japanese must have time; and the structure of the Japanese spoken language seems to favour the habit of thinking slowly, for instance a conventional ejaculation, roughly equivalent to 'Look here now!' which used to preface instructions and commands, is like knocking on a door before you enter so that the inmate may have an opportunity to wake up.

Even so, you must give him leisure to collect his faculties; and, having collected them as a man in the dead of night gropes round half bemusedly for his scattered clothes, it is very possible that, when he finally unbolts the door, he may still meet your request with staring silence. It must repeat itself patiently from beginning to end; and here another trick of Japanese speech enables him yet further to postpone the trial: '*Eto*'—the second syllable a sighing breath: 'Well, well! Let us see. . . .' He strokes his chin. Should your demand be in the least harsh or unexpected, complete paralysis may nail him to the floor.

A quick 'come-back', rapid response, one rarely meets. An agonizing pause must intervene. But just as the Japanese, slow to wrath, are capable of berserk fury once aroused, so once they have firmly grasped a situation, they will devote themselves with endless patience to meeting its needs. Emphatically they are industrious rather than clever; whereas the Chinese, in the ordinary business of life, are cynical, quick-witted but apathetic. The Japanese possess the virtue of perseverance; yet their perseverance has its curious limitations. For so energetic a race they are strangely feminine, and when they collapse it is with awful unexpectedness.

An interesting feature, their collapsability. Maybe the 'pessimism' on which Japanese often dwell has some reference to the sense of inner weakness. Their enthusiasms are exuberant but short-lived; students who to-day fill the lecture room, crowding it to the point of suffocation, tomorrow lose heart and disappear. Bad weather is enough to keep them at home; while a student, at other times abnormally zealous, will excuse himself by 'a slight pain in the head' in a footnote attached to his unfinished essay. Alcohol they can few of them resist; half a glassful of wine or a drain of spirits will completely befuddle a grown man. A drunken Japanese is oddly pathetic, with glistening red cheeks and bleary eyes.

Intoxication separates him from the mass, and it is in the mass that Japanese are estimable. Their virtues are predominantly collective; and one is confronted, when living in Japan, by a type of existence, ways of thought

A HERO OF THE REVOLUTION OF 1863
ON THE KABUKI STAGE

and modes of behaviour now almost extinct in the Western world. It is the psychology, the constitution, of a laborious anthill; one comes to believe—though perhaps this is misleading—that between individual Japanese stretches a much narrower personal gulf than between individual Europeans. So watertight, so rigid their society; so closely does convention bind them together; so brilliantly has their genius for collective effort triumphed over the weakness of separate units.

Yet the system shows signs of falling apart. You cannot pour into the minds of worker-ants a highly individualist philosophy and hope that they will remain unperturbed. Even the Imperial insect at the centre, shut up in the secrecy of his great palace, must before long feel the influence of change. The family, which is the microcosm of the Empire, has already begun to lose its original grasp. But the old system is crafty and tenacious; and the battle of young and old in modern Japan is not confined to the struggle for political freedom. . . . That such a battle is being waged, one cannot doubt; witness the remark of a Japanese to a friend of ours who asked some question about the young. 'As a foreigner,' he explained, shaking his head, 'you probably know more about them than I do.' A complete lack of sympathy and understanding seems to divide the youthful and the middle-aged.

Communism is a mere incident in the revolt. It is true that the transformation of the country has barely touched its underlying mediæval framework; true also, that industrialism grafted on to feudalism has had unpleasant results for many concerned, and that discontent and misery are rife. But these are symptoms and, as usual, enlightened ordinances have brought forth a far more bitter crop.

Education is more productive of discontent than the parasitic growth of political jobbery. Among the educated, restlessness goes deeper; they must fulfil themselves by escaping into the outer world, which the fortunate and the talented immediately do—or come to terms with the ancient hierarchic system, though unfitted for it by every gain in 'Western knowledge'.

Just how deadening and oppressive that system is may be gauged by the fate of returned travellers. Japanese, who have lived too long in Europe, are surrounded when they return to the Japanese world by an air of vague mistrust or overt enmity, which isolates them and makes it difficult to settle down. They want space, they want freedom—both are absent—the permission to go uncriticized their own way. And Japan is as airless and hard to breathe in as an old building filled with whirring modern machinery.

But, for the huge majority, escape is out of the question; hence the charm nowadays exercised by foreign literature. Not only does it give shape with enchanting boldness to all kinds of subversive political theories, but more generally it exhales a breath of freedom such as few Japanese can hope to enjoy. Even the language seems refreshing after their own; and this contrast, considerably to my surprise, was once voiced by a student in his essay, a young man whose behaviour was not ingratiating and usually short and sullen to the point of rudeness: 'I think that the English language', ran his thesis, 'is the expression of the English people as well as the Japanese language is that of the Japanese. The English people are creative like a fountain jumping up towards Heaven eternally. Therefore the English language is always fresh and pure. The Japanese people are rather mechanical like a rat coming out of a hole. Therefore the Japanese language is hesitating. . . .'

The linguistic side of his criticism I cannot vouch for; but I am afraid that his sketch of the Japanese temperament as rat-like and 'rather mechanical' on its chosen path has a certain accuracy, though it is the accuracy of a caricature. At least, that is how it strikes an onlooker, and I have often been reminded of his essay in the bustle of a crowded Japanese town, the little dark shops and muddy back streets, with people slipping secretively to and fro, subdued and oddly purposeless as a swarm of rats running in and out through the passages of a gloomy warren.

Rat-pedestrians, rat-officials and ratty schoolboys; rats must be as pessimistic as the Japanese, and, in spite of everything, as inveterately clannish. The Japanese still worship their native soil; they believe—and cannot rid themselves of the belief—that Japan is the Country of the Gods and to set foot there is to feel its mysterious potency. When Einstein visited Tokyo on his travels, journalists solemnly hinted in the Japanese papers that his life's work might be revolutionized by the contact. No one could contrive to visit Japan without experiencing its semi-divine spell. . . . Was it not founded by the Sun Goddess? The Chinese, who abhor their bellicose neighbours and refer to them laconically as 'the dwarf barbarians', tell a different story of its origin. A profligate Chinese empress, so they say, was deported by her much abused imperial husband and set adrift all alone in a tiny boat. She floated across the narrow Straits of Tsushima and touched Japan, then a forest-covered island, only inhabited by a number of small apes. With these animals the libidinous and lonely Empress soon established an affectionate understanding;

and it was their progeny, adds a Chinese shrugging his shoulders, who first settled the present Japanese Empire.

Thus the Chinese, from their sense of 'effortless superiority', an uncomfortable and badly damaged perch, yet quite broad enough for the average Chinese intellect. The Japanese are mere *parvenus*, they like to insist; while the Japanese reply that their admitted borrowings have been transformed by the peculiar quality of their national genius. Each assertion can be substantiated by evidence; for, though the Japanese are unquestionably inveterate borrowers, it is also true that, since the process first began, they have never failed to give their spoils a distinctive colouring. As individuals they may be shadowy and effaced, but as a people they are strongly idiosyncratic. Every object, once immersed in Japanese life, undergoes immediate crystallization.

It reappears characteristically 'Japanese'. Telegraph poles, modern cinemas and trams—the trams in which at a given signal all those who have not been able to find a seat lurch headlong like a row of human ninepins, then regain their precarious balance with hissing apologies— become as Japanese as stone lanterns and scarlet *torii*—not as pretty but quite as much a part of the scene. Round them, too, convention begins to solidify, tradition and traditional observances to grow up. What at the first glance appears a mongrel civilization, when you know it better proves oddly homogeneous. . . . For modern Japan has contradictory aspects; on one side there is evidence of disruption, of deep discontent with the ancient order, while, on the other a tendency to develop outwards is held in check by the basic conservatism of the race. This plunge and recoil proceeds eternally; and the whole gimcrack fabric as it now stands seems to be maintained in perpetual oscillation. Is the arc through which it moves growing wider, or very gradually will it come at length to rest?

CHAPTER III

THE STAGE

The building may weather the strain, but not its ornaments. All the charm, the 'picturesqueness', of Japanese life, advertised so speciously by Western travellers, has been shivered in the earthquake shock of modernism like some object only unbroken because untouched. It has vanished with the isolation which preserved it. That Japanese culture was at least moribund before the Meiji—if not a mere corpse within its tomb, still fresh-looking while no air could breathe on its features—is suggested by the rapidity with which it has crumbled. As early as 1798, a Japanese writer, when pleading for expansion, declared boldly that cultural growth was at a standstill. The canons which regulated æsthetic feeling were as sterile as the empty protocol of politeness.

Everything becomes conventional in Japan: courtesy, the sense of cleanliness, the feeling for art. Thus, it is a convention to keep the interior of a house clean, to arrange flowers in the ceremonial alcove and to hang certain pictures in a certain way. The outside of a house is another matter; it may be as dishevelled and unprepposses-

UZAEMON

sing as you please. Nor are buildings constructed in the Western style, government offices, universities and schools, considered to be deserving of much nicety; and Japanese, even the most fastidious, are strangely unaffected by squalid surroundings.

So it is in questions of æsthetic taste. But the process of crystallization to which I have referred, though deadening, acts also as a preservative. Nothing could be more slipshod than a Japanese town, with its look of an American frontier settlement, the thick telegraph posts leaning all awry, the low shop fronts masked in corrugated iron. An haphazard supremely philistinian prospect! And yet, here and there, as one comes closer, are little enchanting fragments of good taste, mysteriously left intact by the general havoc: cheap crockery, the printed cotton strips which are sold to be made up as women's sashes, widths of patterned silk for lining sleeves, lacquer bowls and lacquer trays, domestic furniture—the last in smooth-grained white paulownia wood—and all the elegant apparatus of the writing desk.

In such details the Japanese is still an æsthete; but taste, as they are prepared to admit themselves, is less uncommon lower down in the social scale than in the world of enlightened students and busy professors. The pen is superseding the traditional brush—the fountain-pen with a hard characterless nib that robs the Japanese ideogram of its proper fluency; whereas the shopman or the inn-keeper does his accounts, holding a brush gracefully upright between finger and thumb, delicately moistening its point on the hollowed ink-stone, in the attitude of a contemplative Chinese sage.

Most Japanese wear the national dress at home; but the

shopkeeper still wears it in the street, just as his wife retains the traditional native coiffure. Lovely, if absurd, that
coiffure is!—a helmet flattened artfully across the neck in
two broad wing-shaped flanges of pomaded hair, a frontal
piece drawn back circularly from the forehead, the whole
edifice crowned by a huge *chignon*. It dwarfs and oddly
conventionalizes the face; and the face itself, heavily coated
with liquid white, downcast, unsmiling, inexpressive, exquisitely completes the picture of subservient womanhood. . . .

As harmonious is the paraphernalia of masculine fashion. Divided skirts, or baggy trousers, over the kimono
are assumed by middle-class citizens when walking out,
though often dispensed with by the rank and file. Short
coats, which bear a miniature family crest embroidered in
a tiny circle upon the sleeve, made of silk or, during the
warm months, of gauzy tissue, serve as a practical and
easily fitting outer garment; while the kimono, which is
generally brown or grey, admits of a wide range of charming patterns. The *ensemble* is elegant but subdued; Japanese elegance—and this is perhaps its greatest merit—is
usually based on an almost religious care for detail and
likes to express itself by a complete absence of outward
show. The lining should be richer than the robe; spontaneity must be studied as a fine art; and the product of in-
breeding and over-refinement is an air of consummate
rightness in everyday objects. Japanese art was the art of
life: if so many of its creations when brought to Europe
seem unimpressive, trivial and somehow meaningless, it is
no doubt because the secret of Japanese culture was its
domestic and utilitarian quality. The Japanese have been
dubbed 'a people of artists', whereas 'a race of dilettantes'

would be nearer the truth, since it is not the artist whose way of life is most 'artistic' and the genius of Japanese in their later period, during the seclusion of the seventeenth and eighteenth centuries, is best exemplified by the discreet but glowing polish they were able to confer upon the surface of the everyday world. . . .

In arts strictly creative they were poor enough, for creative art is visionary and experimental, and vision and experiment are not matters of taste. Nor can it be said that Western art, though earnestly imitated by the young, has yet helped Japanese artists to a new impulse. Mock-Cézannes, mock-Renoirs and spurious Matisses are turned out with great facility by modern painters, whose enthusiasm is in advance of their real talent. Where art persists, it is as vestige of the old order; but these vestiges, through their hold on popular taste, are even now indisputably alive. They have come drifting down over the muddy waters of change, a floating detached fragment of mediæval Japan.

In the theatre one steps back a hundred years. The Kabuki-za, the home of traditional melodrama, is a large and solid building in a bustling neighbourhood, much bigger and more comfortable than a Western theatre—it has the dimensions of a European opera-house—replete with restaurants, little shops, rooms and passages in which the audience take the air between the acts. The auditorium is well equipped and very spacious, possessing modern tip-up seats and an ugly curtain. Entire families of the more old-fashioned Japanese crowd the floor and fill the galleries as far as the roof.

They are silent, deeply attentive to the play. Three sonorous blows of wood on wood preface the rise of the garish curtain which discovers a long brilliantly lighted stage—twice as long, at a rough guess, as any Western scene—and connected with the rear of the theatre by a raised gang-plank running out upon the left. This is an alternative means of exit; it may also be used as a subsidiary platform, and sometimes, besides the actors who command the stage, there are others who stand perched above the audience, separated from them only by a few feet, entering or leaving through their midst and holding separate colloquies as they go. . . .

A first impression is vaguely of immense sumptuousness. All the costumes worn by Kabuki actors are traditional in colour and design, rich heavy silks and massive brocades set off by such dignity and sense of style that they resemble the lustrous carapaces of splendid insects. Nothing slipshod or tawdrily inconsequent spoils the illusion; actors move deliberately behind the footlights and, when they pause to open a fan or arrange a robe, perform the gesture with so conscious a natural skill that virtuosity itself is put to shame. They are natural in a supernatural key, and the effect is less of naturalism or of symbolism than of another life quite distinct from the life one knows —another world, another sphere of human existence. Their voices, too, though typically Japanese with the ding-dong monotonous rhythm of Japanese speech, have a curious ranting inflection all their own. They roll their eyes dramatically and twist their mouths; they stamp their feet and assume postures of stiff astonishment. . . .

As for the story—that is mysterious and far-away, plot and sub-plot and counter-plot woven together in the most undramatic fashion and tangled up in the most improbable of intrigues. A great deal appears to be happening and not enough; there is little attempt at climax and crescendo, and the little there is trails off into insignificance. Everybody's passions remain at boiling point; but the drama boils and bubbles to slight effect.

Speaking loosely, there are two classes of popular melodrama—plays of comparatively recent origin, which have to do with the later feudal period, its courtesans, dissolute merchants and fierce samurai, and plays which depict the events of an earlier epoch and are inspired by the romantic atmosphere of the ancient No-dance. The former are to some extent naturalistic; and it was one of these that, on a memorable afternoon which extended itself hazily into the evening—we were in the theatre from about five till past eleven—gave me my first experience of the national drama. I left the building with a headache and acute cramp, but with an increased respect for the possibilities of the Japanese genius.

The stage-management would alone have been impressive. Nowhere is crowd-work in the theatre controlled with such efficiency as at the Kabuki-za. Every super plays his part with devoted selflessness, and large groupings produce a finished harmonious pattern that any corps of trained dancers might be proud to achieve. The revolving stage is frequently in operation; and one sees, for instance, an attack on the front of a house—Japanese houses with their boxlike plain interiors offer a special scope for stage design—and then the whole edifice smoothly pivots upon its axis and one sees the occupants escaping through the rear, tumbling out in wild confusion before the marauders.

Or take another example of the same aptitude. It is from a play which I saw that afternoon and introduces two celebrated modern mummers. Uzaemon is a favourite with Tokyo people, a middle-aged man with a long neck, a face at once ugly and attractive and a queer charm in everything he does. He was acting in the part of a rich merchant's son, a dissipated habitué of the Yoshiwara; while Baiko, a veteran of the Japanese stage, wrinkled and hollow-jowled under the powder, impersonated a harum-scarum Japanese beauty, a courtesan or an errant wife—I have forgotten which. Actresses are unknown in the Kabuki-za; and the technique of female impersonation has developed along individual lines. For the actor who interprets feminine roles youth and grace are not necessary adjuncts. Thus Baiko can never have been good-looking and is now over fifty at a conservative estimate. He is qualified by his great experience of the theatre and by his unexampled grasp of female psychology.

Forget the face—it is the mask of an old man, with whitened prominent nose and sagging dewlap—and Baiko at his mirror, tiring his hair, has all the artfulness and insidious modesty of an accomplished charmer. He speaks in a high nasal falsetto voice, which does not imitate so much as subtly caricature the intonation affected by Japanese womanhood. He is coy, fragile-looking, compact of reticences; his movements as he inserts a slender pin, settles a comb, pats in place a lustrous bandeau, peeping from side to side into the glass and sometimes smirking and sometimes pouting at his own image, are delicately, even ludicrously true. He excels in the suggestion of flighty conduct, when his attitude, half impulsive and half distraught, has the drooping exhausted pliancy of a wind-blown chrysanthemum. Or he is gay, a little raffish and rather cunning; or innocent and feather-headed, a young girl. . . .

UZAEMON AS ONE OF THE RONIN IN
'CHUSHINGURA

To return to the episode I have mentioned. The heroine, surrounded by her maids and by a miscellaneous group
of noisy holiday-makers, is on her way home from the
seashore where she has been gathering shells. The party
is good-humoured, the day is warm, and, as they straggle
by in their brightly figured summer kimono, the young
prodigal, escorted by a friend, makes his appearance on
the gangway that crosses the theatre, advancing in the
opposite direction. He is pallid and somewhat shaky after
a debauch; he moves with slightly titubating steps and
carries a small tobacco-pipe in one hand. The hand trem-
bles; his progress is unsteady. But his escort, a large rolling boisterous person, runs against the advance-guard of
the other group, and there is an argument which threatens
to become a scrimmage.

Uzaemon shrinks aside out of harm's way. His nerves
are obviously bad during his 'hang-over', and, in his capacity of degenerate *fils de famille* he is anxious at all costs
to avoid a row. As a piece of comic miming it could
scarcely be better, while as conspicuous is the finished
symmetry of the whole episode—the parties meeting and
jostling on the stage, and the shell-gatherers in laughing
twos and threes strolling back along the causeway across
the audience. The entire incident is perfectly co-ordinated
and, though twenty or thirty actors are concerned, the
spectacle never loses its bright precision and remains as
carefully balanced as a Japanese drawing. It recalls irresis-
tibly a coloured print, some spaciously conceived triptych
by Utamaro with its populace of tall willowy feminine
figures, picnicking or breaking branches from the flowering cherry trees.

The young man encounters the lady in mid-stage. Their

eyes meet unexpectedly but they pass on, among the murmuring and tittering of the delighted maidservants. They look back and again their eyes meet. She continues to drift away from him down the walk; but he pauses, staring blankly as she recedes till one feels that the chance sympathy which exists between them is like a thread growing tauter and more vibrant. . . . From the depths of perturbation he still gazes, and the loose silk overcoat which he is wearing slips slowly, very slowly, from his shoulder, down his arm and, in a rush, on to the floor. He stands rooted, impervious to its loss. . . .

At this point, there was a burst of calling and clapping. The audience, who knew the episode by heart and were interested in the treatment rather than in the story, acclaimed the polished performance of Uzaemon. Kabuki plays bristle with these niceties, and many of the less prosperous theatregoers—stalls cost twelve or thirteen shillings and seats in the dress circle almost as much—crowd in at a specially reduced tariff to see a single act of a famous drama. They derive their interest from an exhibition of pure skill, the actor, an elaborately trained gymnast, is required to surmount some obstacle in a flying leap and come to earth with superb assurance on the further side. His style, his intrepidity, give them pleasure; and no doubt the clumsy realistic pantomime, often substituted for acting on the Western stage, to Japanese must appear extraordinarily insignificant. So tenacious, even in the present enlightened epoch, are habits of traditional æstheticism!

The actor is a stylist above all else. With few exceptions the performers of to-day are descended from well-known theatrical clans which have produced actors, in direct line, for a hundred years. They have appeared on the stage since they could speak and, though the modern theatrical community is no longer cut off from the world at large as happened during the Tokungawa Shogunate when they were rigorously confined to certain districts, they still form a very close corporation, largely unaffected by the spirit of change. They are proud, it would seem, of their professional privacy; and, while the English actor likes it to be known that he, too, is a man among other men and attends the 'best' parties and is fond of golf, the Japanese is content to remain an artist—a specialist, that is to say, in his own medium.

As an artist, nothing he does is unconsidered. The training he has undergone from earliest childhood is not confined to the technique of imitation. Crude mimicry is the least of his accomplishments, for he has learned that the career which he has adopted should absorb every atom of his personal strength—that he must be an actor when he walks or uses his fan as essentially as when he is playing a star part. Each gesture, then, is gradually perfected, with the result that a group of Japanese mummers, engaged in some unimportant scene—sitting around the fire-box, for example, and tapping out their pipes against its edge— lend the operation an air of suave completeness that distinguishes it from the practice of mere realism.

They are fortunate, maybe, in human subjects. The centripetal bias of the Japanese, their conventionalism and deep regard for the established, have imprinted on every facet of their common life the stamp of a unique family-feeling. Their history has made them what they are; it has so attuned individual to individual that, as happens in self-centred domestic groups, communication can dispense with explicit utterance. Thus sincerity is superfluous in the social sphere. Since a message can be eloquently conveyed by a flicker of an eyelash or a change of tone, there is no need of that scandalous and brutal frankness that, for a Japanese, mars the intercourse of Western peoples. But these very limitations and shortcomings are to the actor a positive advantage; synthesized and transfigured by his art, they are eminently neat, colourful and characteristic.

Reminiscences of the graphic arts abound. It is not only that one's acquaintance with coloured prints has already made one free of the Japanese stage and familiarized one with costumes that are still worn, but more subtly, the technique of the moving spectacle seems to hark back to the grace of the fixed design. The same implacable samurai stalk the theatre; one sees again as they sit down or draw their swords—those swords in elegantly curving lacquer scabbards that project from the kimono like an animal's brush—and fling off the right hand sleeve to clear the sword-arm, an attitude one has elsewhere admired in terms of draughtsmanship. A Japanese, whether he walks or squats or stands, is beautifully, sometimes irritatingly, true to type.

To remain true is the measure of Japanese heroism; the most famous and best-loved dramatic themes are based on the mediæval code of loyalty which demanded the sacrifice of the individual to his obligations. That obligation might be senseless or worse than senseless. *Chushingura*, the play of the Forty-Seven Ronin who bloodily avenge their master's death—he had been condemned to rip out his own bowels as a punishment for brawling in the Shogun's palace—elicits deep emotion when it is produced. This abstract vendetta has become a classic; while Benkei, the hero of *Kanjincho*, is almost as celebrated as the leader of the Ronin. He, too, was a victim of chivalric duty, though his sacrifice was accomplished in another way.

He laid hands on—actually struck—his feudal lord. Yoshitsune, the brother of the reigning Shogun, had been proscribed and was fleeing for his life. His retainers, headed by the faithful Benkei, had disguised themselves in the garb of warrior monks, and Yoshitsune, that the disguise might be more thorough, accompanied them as a servant carrying their baggage. They were intercepted at a pass by the Shogun's officer—a part which was taken, when I saw the play, by the illustrious Sadanji Ichikawa, *doyen* of the modern Japanese stage and renowned for his dignity in classic roles. I see him now advancing amid applause: he glides forward as quietly as an automaton, for the voluminous pleated trousers, which encase his legs, are so long, in the court-fashion of the period, that they entirely muffle his feet and he walks inside them, a yard of empty trouser trailing behind. Enormous drooping sleeves cover his arms; on his head, a huge bean-shaped varnished cap is secured by white cords under the chin which terminate in two heavy silken tassels. To move in such regalia must be a feat; but Ichikawa glides up with immense aplomb and seats himself magnificently on a tiny chair, ruffling out his fabulous plumage as he does so and spreading it around him in the opulent folds that tradition requires.

Equally splendid is the retinue of warrior-monks. They file in over the gang-plank on the left, Yoshitsune lagging a few paces behind. He wears a wide hat and carries a staff; they carry rosaries, fans, are girt with swords and have long hair bunched thickly across their shoulders. Loose coats of a resplendent dark purple, kimono in boldly chequered tartan silk, broad trousers which resemble divided skirts and hang down to within an inch or two of the floor, are topped by small caps like black birettas, settled precariously on the forehead between the eyes. They march in, then halt to consider their plan. Shall they trust to audacity and rush the gate, or try what can be done by dissimulation?

For the moment, it seems there will be a skirmish. Benkei and the Shogun's officer are face to face; and the officer, having risen from his stool, whips back his sleeve to bare his arm and crouches with his hand upon his sword. In spite of his silken trappings he is incredibly agile; the two men, both grasping their narrow sword-hilts, manœuvre as they wait for the other to draw. They perform a kind of shifting, stamping dance that, so strange are their habiliments and bellicose postures, gives them the look of birds sparring for a mate, two truculent ruffled cockbirds with swollen plumage who prance from foot to foot and work their necks, bright beady eyes fastened upon their rival. The drama now becomes a miniature ballet; stooping shapes veer and sidestep across the stage, feet stamping and their resemblance to fighting birds enhanced by huge sleeves like outspread wings which flap and sway to the slow cadence of their movements.

Warily they move apart and their feathers subside. The parley which ensues is long and tedious—typical of such dialogues on the Japanese stage where brisk action is interspersed with endless colloquies, the protagonists sitting as immobile as painted posts. At last the Shogun's officer puts a query. If they are indeed monks as they pretend, out collecting funds for a new temple, is there any subscription list that they can show? Benkei is disconcerted

KOSHIRO MATSUMOTO AS BENKEI

but not at a loss. Producing a scroll from the bosom of his robe, he improvises an interminable catalogue of imaginary donors. He throws in some references to the religious life, calculated to complete the effect of verisimilitude.

This is a moment for which the audience have been waiting. When Benkei has finished his brilliant impromptu, there is an outburst of enthusiasm in the distant gallery. The officer, though impressed, is far from satisfied. He calls back the pretended monks whom he has allowed to go; and Benkei, with a desperate stroke of guile, affects to fall foul of his disguised master, declares that he is a bad servant and strikes him angrily. No subterfuge could be more awful in its implications: the liege has publicly assaulted his feudal lord. And the officer, moved by the enormity of Benkei's daring, by the devoted self-sacrifice which it entails—it is as if a Brahmin should slaughter a sacred cow—grants permission for the whole party to go their way. Then Benkei kneels at Yoshitsune's feet; he has saved his master, but his own life is at an end. The nobleman forgives him and—second prodigy—extends his arm and clasps the hand of his faithful guardian.

The audience's emotion is at fever-heat. . . . I have included a brief summary of *Kanjincho*, partly for the light it casts on the Japanese mind and partly as a famous example of the classic drama. It will be understood that, with a background of such stories and an outlook still predominantly mediæval, a Japanese may be somewhat beyond his depth in *Othello* or *Hamlet* or *Coriolanus*. The subtlety which he asks of the presentation, he does not expect of the theme which is portrayed; and under the lacquer-surface of æsthetic nicety he looks for a solid basis of traditional sentiment.

CHAPTER IV

ACTORS AND DANCERS

K*anjincho* was originally adapted from a No-play and, like many other Kabuki dramas, it appears to have more in common with the dance than with the drama understood as a literary medium. Dancing in Japan is still spontaneous. Thus, in the country—at the feast of departed souls, when lighted lanterns are set afloat upon the lake and come glimmering under the piers of the wooden bridge, drawn down by the waterfall beyond the rapids as it plunges from a rocky shelf towards the plain—the village people and the foreigners' servants collect at night and dance endlessly round the high musicians' platform, two concentric rings meeting and parting, with a slow sideways step and deliberate gestures which seem to appeal to the enormous fellowship of the dead. . . .

A Japanese dance inclines to gravity and deliberation, whether it be the dance before an obscure local shrine or a *pas seul*, behind harsh electric footlights, by Kikugoro, the best known of modern dancers. Its rhythm is perceptible but very slow—a quality which may ultimately become attractive but is at first somewhat baffling and monotonous. For most Westerners, the idea of graceful move-

ment is connected with a certain idea of speed. We are apt
to recognize the essential beauty of a dance not so much in
the separate positions of the performer as in the invisible
line that gathers them into one—in the cursive rather than
in the static aspect. What our eyes follow is a subtly involved pattern marked out by perpetually moving hands
and feet. Posture flows so rapidly into posture; the effect
of the dancing is hardly distinct from the effect of the
music; and the whole impression, by being always a little
confused, is apt to suggest more than it really states.

But now imagine on the stage of the Kabuki-za the first
appearance of Kikugoro from the wings. The stage itself
is enormous and quite empty, except for the orchestra
squatting motionless among their instruments. . . . Suddenly, saluted by a roar of welcome, he runs forth—almost
scuttles—into the light, with bent knees and faltering feminine steps, timorous and irresistible at the same time, a
perfect embodiment of frightened seductive womanhood,
as though he were blown in like a feather or a dead leaf,
his face, wonderfully dwarfed by the blue-black coiffure,
swaying backwards and forwards while he moves, his
skirts hissing and bundling around his feet, his sandals
pattering audibly across the boards.

It would seem, that the intention with which he sets out
is to impress us not by any parade of strength, but by the
fluidity, the gracious limpness, of his entire demeanour.
From this beginning he proceeds—but very gradually—
to develop the elaborate rhythms of the dance. He unwinds, as one unwinds a skein of silk, the fragile unbroken
strand that threads his postures, a clue always there but
so transparent that a Western eye, in losing and picking it
up again, grows bewildered long before the end; sleeves

flapping, fan opening, coiffure bending, all underlined by the acid music of smitten strings.

His pendant sleeves, pliable and loose, long enough nearly to sweep the ground, are managed with consummate delicacy and rightness, a ghostly extension of the arm and hand that move them, as they flick over in a rapid glistening arc or droop and sway like foliage against the wind. Instead of a body which dances inside its trappings, here is a dancer whose voluminous clinging robes are the expression, the final triumph, of his virtuosity. Though Western dancing—and Western art in every form—cannot forget the splendour of the naked animal, nakedness from the point of view of Eastern races is unseemly, unappetizing, a trifle absurd. In pornography, perhaps, but not in art, the naked human body may have its charm; and dancers, unconcerned to show their muscles, delight us by the fold and flow of heavy stuffs.

Among the Chinese, this principle is carried further, and the body as far as possible melts away, leaving only the soft outline of its dress. Mei-lan-fang, at his suavest and most accomplished, has a gracefulness so exaggeratedly inhuman that every posture suggests a miracle of calligraphy, produced by a single sweep of some clever brush rather than supported on a crude framework of bone and sinew. He is *all* dress, like the ladies of Chinese porcelains, bedizened head, pointed expressive nails, and under them a mere wraith of floating drapery, a ghost, an emanation of spirit force drawn upward by the shrill ascent of his own song.

Less ethereal are the posturings of Kikugoro. Mei-lan-fang in private life is slight and willowy; but the Japanese dancer, when he appears in ordinary garb, is revealed as

a short and solid person with thick bandy legs and muscular arms. His dancing, for all its characteristic delicacy,
has a precision and a degree of accomplishment which are
wholly masculine. Great strength and the devoted labour
of many years have gone into the proper handling of his
heavy robe, of the fan or the umbrella which he carries.
Not one robe, but often four or five, provide an obstacle
which his skill must overcome. . . . I am thinking particularly of the so-called Heron Dance, when he slips free of
one kimono after another like an insect brilliantly emerging from successive chrysales, reborn, as he steps clear, in a
new mood.

He is the phantom of a young girl, crazed with love; he
is also a heron, and in the stately plumage of the bird postures the hopeless melancholy of old desire, beneath moon-
light which is shining vaguely through the mist. Japanese
art and the Japanese temperament are full of phantoms.
From the earliest period, this active and excitable race
have relished dim woolgathering among the shades, have
talked of ghosts and taken pleasure in quiet melancholy,
imagining the intense loneliness of the world to come.
Loneliness, if one can judge from artistic evidence, must
be an obsession, a haunting fear of the Japanese. There
are the 'hungry ghosts' of a famous painted scroll; and
there are the forlorn children, tormented after death, who
require the special comfort of a benign Jizo. A lonely
race; and the rhythm of the Heron Dance is of loneliness
pitched in a phantasmal key, purified and attenuated by
the power of art till it is no more than the lyric abstraction
of real suffering.

The music, though not important in itself, combines
admirably with the plaintive measures of the ballet. Sami-

sen music, melancholy at its most cheerful, has for such occasions an unbearably appealing note. Bitter-sweet at its sweetest to the Western taste, it acquires a poignancy that plays direct upon the nerves, wailing gushes that have no origin and no sequel but expire suddenly like the sound of wind in an autumn reed-bed, sharp cries that quaver off into utter silence and low vibrations that murmur lengthily within the ear. This accompaniment, to the untrained foreign listener, makes promises which it very seldom keeps. It is exciting but seldom or never satisfying, prodigal of hints which drop stillborn into the brain, of dead-ends and barren clues which lead him nowhere. Similarly the dance, however delightful at a given moment, seems to be lacking in any obvious connecting line. The eye, which follows the dancer as he moves, fixes a posture and hurries on to catch the next.

A series of postures, separate shapes along a frieze; I remember the fluttering dance of the ghostly heron and his last entry, the crescendo of the whole dance, when Kikugoro stands forth all in white—a heavy white silk kimono with scarlet linings—hooded in white, rather squat, with his huge umbrella, but giving off an odd phosphorescent gleam, insect-like or grub-like in his pallid thickness, slowly pivoting, slowly sinking towards the ground, while the translucent disc of the paper sunshade slowly revolves. . . .

A second dance, which I saw a little later, displayed a different aspect of the dancer's skill. *Kagami Shishi*—in other words the Mirror Lion—demands vigorous miming and great boldness in execution. This ballet, one of the most difficult of dramatic themes, concerns a ritual dance in the household of a certain daimyo, which was performed every

KIKUGORO IN THE HERON DANCE

year by a maid-in-waiting who danced holding a venerable lion-mask. Kikugoro takes the part of a young girl supposedly not accomplished enough for such an honour. Her embarrassment at being obliged to assume the role provides him with a characteristic entry; he palpitates into the centre of the stage, almost hugging himself in an ecstasy of naive alarm, the hair-trinkets trembling and sparkling upon his coiffure, while he essays with downcast eyes his opening steps.

A Japanese friend, when commenting on this passage, pointed out its 'decidedly erotic' charm. Alas, that in matters of erotic taste there should be no reconciling Eastern and Western sympathies. A white visage splendidly helmeted with black horsehair, a rich robe, gravely beckoning pendant sleeves, plump forearms and small hands that are soft but sinuous, enchant our eyes but leave our senses undisturbed. The hands particularly fascinate attention, for Japanese hands, even hands which are worn and rough, have a character and flexibility all their own. Few features are more expressive than the hand—those long hands with curiously swollen finger-joints, cold-looking, bloodless and finely made, which you catch sight of in pictures by Botticelli, or the princely hands immortalized by Van Dyck, their round backs and tapering pale digits.

The Japanese hand bends backward upon its wrist with a suppleness at once arresting and a trifle horrid. The short fingers, too, which seem so clumsy, can deflect from the large palm at the strangest angles. Young women and young girls of every class have the plump curled-up fingers and rounded wrists that are conventionalized in the gallant creations of Utamaro. Thus the cushioned curve, which swells beneath the thumb, meets directly the soft bulge of the under-arm. Fine attachments, showing the delicacy of the joint, are neither cultivated nor admired by the Japanese. But these hands, however inelegant by Western standards, are capable of a supreme elegance once set in motion.

For the entire hand then, like a fleshy calyx, opens miraculously at the appeal of a subtle rhythm. The fact that a dancer or a dancing girl shows of the physical self the hands and the hands only—if one excepts the impassive whitened face, lips marked by a single dab of rouge—gives to their movement an almost personal existence, as though they formed a last connection with human life. . . . Kikugoro, in the dance of the Mirror Lion, lets them express at first a naive girlish trepidation, taking courage as the character of the part develops. A pair of butterflies now join him on the stage, little gaudily painted creatures in stiff trappings; while the lion-spirit which inhabits the ancient mask slides gradually along the performer's extended arms.

There is a double climax: the dancer, lion-possessed, is whirled in a brilliant flurry from the lighted stage, to come leaping back a lion in every point. . . . Not, it must be added, the King of Beasts with his look of an ageing nineteenth century statesman as the Romantic artists brought him into vogue, but the Chinese animal, ferocious and yet benevolent, who frolics among the peonies that are his emblem or rolls tenderly the savage kittens he has whelped; not the constitutional monarch whom Landseer painted, but an Eastern emperor in bulky trousers of thick brocade. The animal face, barred boldly in black and white, is set off by a fierce explosion of white mane which covers his shoulders and sweeps behind him on to the ground.

He rushes forward. His previous avatar was all feminine, and all bestial is the figure he has now assumed. Then
it was the shuddering quality of subservient womanhood,
of the Japanese woman with her artfully turned-in steps,
now astraddle, bowed down by his heavy mane, he flat-
tens himself like a cat about to spring. His knees are wide
apart, and the painted mask rents ponderously on shoulders hunched and arms akimbo. Very direct; but there is
no attempt at naturalism. The fierce concentrated play-
fulness of the feline race lends the imaginary creature
its spirit but not its form—a lion as the lion-nature
might develop if it were transplanted to the envigorating
world of myth. An ability to look beyond the appearance
is shared by the artist and those who watch him. Many
children have this imaginative aptitude, and it is noticeable how even in Western countries it is only lost as the
mind loses its maidenhood and the child begins to see
through the vision of others. . . .

The Japanese luckily are still childish—those, at least,
who visit the Kabuki-za. A new public, of course, is being formed; in Japan, too, the mechanic is a common type,
the young man who is happiest among engines and wears
his overalls as the badge of modern chivalry. Realism is
the atmosphere he breathes and, since there are many gar-
ages in Tokyo, many taxis, many hurtling jangling lorries,
one is inclined to exaggerate his present importance. But
the mechanical view of life has still far to go; and it is not
until one visits the Kabuki-za that one realizes the per-
manence of the old tradition. Kabuki is a middle-class
entertainment and retains its public of old-fashioned
bourgeoisie.

The No-dance is aristocratic in origin; and, whereas the audience at the Kabuki theatre is prosperous, colourful and well dressed—among the crowd you catch sight of budding geisha, little girls of thirteen and fourteen, their heads sparkling with ornament like Christmas trees—No attracts very much the same assemblage as is to be found in London at the staidest sort of concert. Most carry the score under their arms; comfort or discomfort mean nothing to them, and the whole body of the theatre up to the stage—which projects as in the Elizabethan playhouse, beneath a separate roof raised on wooden pillars—is divided into a multitude of tiny pens, squares of matting without back-rest or support.

Six hours is the usual length of the performance, and during that time one watches a number of different plays. At the rear of the roofed stage behind the actors a large pine tree is painted across the wall, a covered gallery which extends upon the left providing the usual means of exit and entry. Scenery of the Western sort there is none. The chorus files noiselessly on to the stage and squats in a double row, stiff and dignified. They strike up, and a gush of wailing melody sweeps out over the heads of the serried audience.

Two musicians hold small gourd-shaped drums. The first perches his instrument between neck and shoulder, and thuds it with the flat of his open hand; the second wears a thimble upon his finger which he raps down to mark the cadence of the chanting. The sound produced has little resonance to a Western ear—a rap, sharp and distinct, nailing the rhythm. A single bamboo flute, which completes the orchestra, whistles now and then with painful shrillness.

That is all; the hoarse chanting of the chorus, directed by the occasional solos of the chorus leader, evoke time and situation and dramatic mood—mountains, the vicinity of some temple, a deserted garden, in accordance with the theme. Vague and ghostly; the action of a No play often requires a ghost or demon presence, and the dim music sobs and gnashes from the stage, like wind interminably wailing in a ruined house. . . . It is monotonous, melancholy and nerve-racking. Very slowly at the end of the covered walk a masked and stealthy phantom now appears. Very slowly, while the chorus continues chanting, it glides forward till it has gained the centre of the stage.

At this point, the students with whom I had come referred me to the papers on my knee. Each of them had written for my benefit a neat synopsis of two plays we were to watch. 'The Goddess of the Mountains', they whispered helpfully. . . . A cascade of disordered silvery hair was brushed back from a contorted demon face, pathetic, horrible and ludicrous at the same time. One is apt to exaggerate first impressions; but the No dancer, slipping silently on to the stage, with his peculiar gliding movements and demonic mask, as the chorus wavered up to a plangent crescendo, did, in fact, convey an idea of unearthly grief.

That movement, that peculiar gliding gait, is essential to the technique of the No theatre. The performers, shod in digitated socks—white *tabi*, the ordinary footwear of men and women—never lift their soles from the polished boards. They stir as silently, as regularly, as if on castors; they glisten forward inch by inch over the floor, immaterial, ghostlike and subdued. . . . To this effect much is added by the mask. Demons have distorted scowling features and long manes of hair, red or grey; old men humorous wrinkles and shaggy eyebrows; while young girls, whether in the spirit or in the flesh, are furnished with an expressionless white oval, blank and bewildered looking, the very epitome of sheltered ignorance.

The masks are too small for the dancers' heads. They do not fit over them closely as one would expect, but stand out with no attempt at absolute realism as though they formed the visor of a helmet. Faces, then, are somewhat smaller than human size; while the body bulks large in its brocaded vestments. Stiff robes with wide sleeves are generally worn, so voluminous that the effect is almost square. The dancer seems at once very massive and preternaturally light as he glides along. . . .

'Goddess of the Mountains' murmured the student at my elbow. I gathered—I forget how or why—that she was an embodiment of frustrate sexual yearning. It may be that I was wrong; it scarcely matters—for what counted was the apparition as it advanced, using a gnarled and ancient bough to support its steps, in a stiffly splendid robe of brocaded silk. Colours here are quieter than in Kabuki, rust red, dark green or sober purple. The goddess moved so slowly into view that she seemed to be crossing the frontiers of visibility, to be gradually materializing as we watched. When she spoke it was in a plangent soughing sing-song that rose to a compulsive chant and died away—as a storm-wind dies away or the noise of an avalanche.

A long silence; characteristic of the No dance is the extreme deliberation which marks its progress and the silence and immobility into which it lapses. Very often the dancers on the stage remain motionless for long peri-

A NŌ DANCER BEING PREPARED TO
MAKE HIS ENTRY

ods together. The chorus, too, is silent and utterly immobile. Only the drummer gives vent to a single cry,
repeated until one writhes with exasperation. *A-a-a-a* he
shrills out on an ascending scale; sharply his thimbled
finger strikes the drum. *A-a-a-a*—once more he repeats
his whoop, and once more his finger crashes against the
instrument. . . .

Yes, the No play has its *longueurs*, one must admit. But
from tedium rises the dawn of understanding. This performance is not intended to amuse; it makes no concession
to popular taste, but strikes direct at the root of æsthetic
pleasure. For a Japanese there is subtle satisfaction in the
drum-beats which accentuate the fall of the verse, harsh
and cruelly monotonous as they may seem. Incidentally,
their reiteration becomes hypnotic; and No, like other
products of the Japanese mind, is very primitive and very
sophisticated at the same moment. The queer hypnotic
spell of a religious ceremony has been elaborated by all
the artifices of conscious æstheticism.

The result is both spontaneous and thought-out. Seami,
the greatest Japanese No master, quoted and translated by
Arthur Waley in his preface to a brilliant volume of trans-
lations, throws some light on its philosophic background.
The dramatist was also a student of Zen Buddhism, and
the word *yugen*, or 'what lies beneath the surface', indicating all that is finest in the art of No, was derived from his
knowledge of Zen literature. 'It means . . . the subtle, as
opposed to the obvious; the hint, as opposed to the statement. It is applied to the natural grace of a boy's movements, to the gentle restraint of a nobleman's speech and
bearing. "When notes fall sweetly and flutter delicately to
the ear", that is the *yugen* of music. The symbol of yugen

is "a white bird with a flower in its beak". "To watch the sun sink behind a flower-clad hill, to wander on and on in a huge forest with no thought of return, to stand upon the shore and gaze after a boat that goes hid by far-off islands, to ponder on the journey of wild geese seen and lost among the clouds"—such are the gates to *yugen*.'[1]

Perhaps *yugen* might be rendered as 'overtone'. At all events, it is the quality most prized, this spontaneity that is the product of deliberate art, a kind of bloom preserved intact by careful culture. Certainly it has nothing to do with realism; 'in imitation there should be a tinge of the "unlike". For if imitation be pressed too far it encroaches on reality and ceases to give an impression of likeness.' The pleasure it affords depends on the individual; 'if you look deeply into the ultimate essentials of this art, you will find that what is called "the flower" has no separate existence. Were it not for the spectator who reads into the performance a thousand excellences, there would be no "flower" at all. The Sutra says "Good and ill are one; villainy and honesty are of like kind". Indeed, what standard have we whereby to discern good from bad? We can only take what suits the need of the moment and call it "good".'

No, then, is predominantly subjective and something of the mysterious charm that it exerts may be due to this absence of specific appeal. The spectator is not 'entertained' in the ordinary sense; but the simplicity and bareness of its art—verse and prose with a meagre rhythmical accompaniment, slow noiseless gestures and stamping feet—give his imagination an unexampled freedom, like the blank margin round one of Mallarmé's later poems.

1 Waley: The Nō Plays of Japan. Allen & Unwin. 1921.

Immobility and silence are made significant; and Seami, in classifying No, mentions a third type which is purely intellectual; 'song, dance, mimic and rapid action are all eliminated, emotion as it were springing out of quiescence. This is called "frozen dance".'

CHAPTER V

THE PUPPET THEATRE

What perils have beset Japanese art! That 'flower' which its critics so often recognize—which they have recognized, one sometimes feels, where it does not exist—breathes a perfume slightly stupefying for all its fragrance. Every art seems to assume in its maturity the attitude of a man inhaling a flower; it grows intoxicated on the essence of its own achievement. Very soon the possibility of true creation is arrested by a kind of narcissistic trance. Art changes to ritual, and faith to dogma; secrecy and sanctity win the day. The artist becomes an initiate, a hierophant; thus No, subtle and fascinating as it still is, produces a certain aroma of pious snobism which would be insufferable were it less exquisitely combined.

Unlike the flamboyant melodrama, it does not flourish, but is kept alive by amateurs and dilettanti; while the Marionettes, once rivals of Kabuki, are reduced to a last stronghold in squalid Osaka. There the art of the puppet masters is still preserved. . . . On the right of the stage sit two figures, the man who recites—or intones—the story, squatting formally at a red lacquer desk, and the musician

who holds an ivory plectrum and accompanies him upon
the tingling samisen. Three shapes occupy the stage,
human-faced, inhumanly attenuated, smaller than life.
These are dolls, the Osaka marionettes, not marionettes of
the European kind, for they are less agile and far more
expressive, and behind each doll crouches its attendants,
hooded in black, wearing black mittens or black gloves.

No strings and little visible machinery; but into the
back of the marionette's capacious sleeve the chief manipulator has slipped his hand. His forefinger passes, when
it is necessary, through a ring on the under side of the
puppet's wrist. If the puppet is to pick up some object,
the manipulator quite simply does it for him, unfolding
the puppet's fan, drawing his sword—an absence of arti-
fice which curiously heightens the impression; the puppets
seem to exist with their own life but to be dependant by
some puzzling freak of circumstance on the black-hooded
helots who support them. The effect, indeed, is vivid
enough to inspire discomfort. There is something a trifle
vicious about the dolls, their disproportionately small heads
and long bodies, the petulant quivers of animation with
which they seem to be struggling against the ministrants.

At first they scarcely move; but as the story-teller tumbles out his words, using that raucous recitative, plangent
and bombastic at the same time, to which one becomes
accustomed in the Japanese theatre, they begin to twitch
irregularly into life. A head turns, a hand stirs; and very
soon they are deploying all the mannerisms of a full-sized
Kabuki actor. And the conventions of the popular stage,
far from losing, seem to gain a new significance. The
world of frowning courtiers and fierce samurai—often
somewhat wearisome on a larger scale—is admirably

suited to the puppet genius. These spitfire dolls lend it a fresh charm; they suggest a race immemorially aristocratic, grown so weak that it depends for its survival on the existence of a breed of giant slaves. . . . The comedy would be deprived of half its fascination if the veiled attendants, resembling executioners, inquisitors or hierophants of some Satanic cult, were not continually moving in the background. With anonymous and patient skill they smooth out and arrange a brocaded robe. Two puppets are intent over a draughts board, and, while it is the servant whose fingers hold the pieces, one feels that he is merely anticipating his master, the imperious and ill-tempered homunculus who dislikes but cannot dispense with his intervention.

Then the eyebrows of the puppet rise. Poised in mid-air, black-gloved fingers—above them a white narrow paw—are hesitating towards some doubtful move. The interrogative flicker of those eyebrows, the nod of uneasy cogitation! But the piece slams down; the game proceeds —a pantomime which synthesizes without caricaturing the gestures of a Japanese draughts player. For here, as upon the adult stage, it is not gesture crudely imitated which counts. It is the spirit, the rhythmic essence of a movement. Separate movements have an harmonious unity; each of them is a separate composition, from the audience's point of view a distinct feat. The actor needs his seconds like an athlete, hence the attendants, humble and black-masked, who during pauses in the action dress, undress and refurbish the live comedian; hence the silent self-effacing doll-servants who, emerging only waist-high from the stage, exist vicariously in the brilliance of their puppets.

During the space of two hours, the story-teller has been changed four times; a man with a large mobile mouth and a strong voice; a younger man with round rosy cheeks; an old man so flushed and congested-looking that, in the expressive frenzy of his chant, he mimics an apoplectic seizure; finally, a grey-haired veteran who makes a deep bow and is welcomed by loud applause. The samisen players, too, are changed. Their music, which resembles in its effect the twanging of an agitated nerve, breaks out where the story is most dramatic. The player utters a cry; his ivory plectrum claws the strings. The teller is rocking to and fro; and the marvellous history of St. Nichiren unfolds itself among miracles and portents, a wild hurricane throbbing from the wings, the puppets, interrupted in their draughts game, adopting positions of statuesque astonishment, as a trunkless head flutters across the stage, balancing nimbly at the tip of a long rod. . . .

Later, there is an accomplished crowd scene. It is on the seashore and a throng of weeping peasants crowd around the persecuted saint. Clad in blue and biscuit-coloured robes, he is almost twice as high as his disciples. They are dingier, more rudimentary in build. Constables beat them back and their desperation is ludicrous and pathetic. An old woman keeps thrusting herself forward. She tumbles prostrate; the saint is led away. . . . Here again one is reminded of the Kabuki stage. Nothing is haphazard or left to chance; and the air of completeness that distinguishes the entire spectacle seems to arise from the devoted labour of all concerned.

The humblest handler of the humblest doll never flags. The gravity with which he puts it through its paces, making it squat, lift its arm, turn its head, is as impressive as the dignity of the story-teller, dressed in a square tabard of blue brocade worn over a dark silk kimono, who sits on a low dais to the right, sometimes refreshing himself from a small teacup near his hand. The audience is attentive and subdued. Among Japanese the capacity for common enjoyment is no less marked than the capacity for common endeavour; and the audience, like the actors whom they watch, appear to be animated during the play by a single spirit.

They experience the same emotion to the same degree. How absolutely their personal differences are often sunk can be observed at the other end of the æsthetic scale, for instance in the festival of a local shrine. Suddenly the whole neighbourhood is *en fête*; tall platforms spring up at the street corners, swathed in strips of red and white bunting; little altars are arranged in empty shops, and paper lanterns dangle down every by-way. There are processions, a crowd of children hauling a drum, a beflowered bullock-cart, men chanting, a priest on horseback. Then the 'god-house' begins to go its rounds, accompanied by a noisy mob of devotees.

All day long it jigs excitedly through the streets, a tabernacle like the Jewish Ark of the Covenant, black and gilt, looped with heavy purple cords, its conical roof surmounted by a gilded phœnix. Lacquered shafts support it on either side; and perhaps a dozen or two dozen young men take turns in carrying it high upon their shoulders. Their thick muscular calves are brown and naked; they have white socks, white drawers above the knee, short blue coats stamped with a large monogram and loose 'sweat-cloths' knotted about their foreheads. Sometimes their cheeks are plastered with paint. They are members of a fraternity or guild, and, not content with merely carrying the shrine, perform a perpetual shuffling dance, stamping and uttering a hoarse cry that sets the rhythm of their rambling mazy progress.

Two staccato syllables, long and short; bent knees work feverishly to the refrain, the bearers, who form a monstrous human centipede as they lean inward against the massive lacquered poles, letting their enthusiasm invade them from top to toe. They are drunk, literally reel, with religious gaiety, and the shrine, like a table during a seance, very soon takes advantage of their exaltation, dipping and plunging, slanting and lurching to left or right, staggering round again to face the way it has come.

The bearers are uproarious yet a trifle dazed. No doubt they are plied with rice wine during halts; but violent exercise usually works off the effect of drink, and the intoxication, under which they most of them seem to labour, is very largely of the spirit and the nerves. They are drunk with the common impulse, the common rhythm, swaying back and leaning their necks against the shaft, eyes half closed in a sheer rapture of self-abandonment, while the sweat glistens upon foreheads and bare legs. . . .

From far away you hear the monotonous croaking chant; and often out of a side street or narrow lane, across a thoroughfare crowded and jangling with Western traffic, the centipede bursts eccentrically into view, and goes plunging and curvetting between the trams. It takes no thought of place and suitability. Detached members leap behind and prance before; it spins about and, with a diagonal desperate dash, flings itself in the path of an approaching vehicle. It is saved. . . . A nimble devoted gendarme, his tinny sword slapping his buttocks as he runs, elevates an imperious cotton glove. Civilization draws up with grinding brakes; the Ark of the Covenant jigs aside on a safer tangent.

PART III

PEKING

CHAPTER I

THE RIVER

Japan has a cumulative effect. Either the sufferer sinks into a deep lethargy from which it is possible he may never quite come round; or the drug, as it penetrates his system, acts as an intense irritant on every nerve. Then the people, the landscape, smells and noises, aggravate his malady hour by hour. The mere sight of his assembled students or dawdling colleagues rouses him to a fresh outburst of nervous spleen. . . .

Such a condition may excuse a shade of hyperbole, and, looking back through the pages of an old notebook, I see that an 'overwhelming relief' was recorded the day we left Japan, bound for China during the short Spring vacation. From Tokyo we took the night train to Kobe, and I remember that, as we ran into Osaka, a thin sulphurous fog had veiled its outskirts, which gave some figures on an embankment near the line and the arches of an unfinished iron bridge, stilting across a wide and fenny river, a ghostly mournful beauty in the half-light. . . . Industrialism needs murk to lend it interest; but the sun had pierced the mist when we reached Kobe, and the big concrete warehouses along the quay stood up jagged and gaunt around the harbour, where wrinkled wavelets, scudding before the breeze, slapped and shivered against the hulls of anchored ships.

We weighed anchor in the early afternoon, and next day were still threading the Inland Sea. The air had a delicious chilly smoothness; while over the water, lilac-coloured in the dawn, the ribbed sails of fishing boats drove by, betwixt the steamer and a sheer volcanic island which rose marvellous and uninhabited from the depths. A second island, when we had passed Shimonosekei and were ploughing the rougher surface of the China Sea, has also somehow fixed itself upon my mind—a mass of rock without landing place or beach, one of those memorable and melancholy scraps of earth that have no existence and no meaning except for navigators; dark cliffs veined white by the bursting swell which tosses its spume far up the cavernous gullies, overhead a poor covering of bleached grass, a few trees nipped and flattened by the wind.

But on the horizon the promised land had come in view—China, the coastline of Shantung, pale hills, dry and dead-looking, in many folds, and behind them the sharp teeth of a snowy range which concluded an immense foreground of tumbling sea, yellowish and thick along the side, growing yellower as the distant shore approached.

It approached, then appeared to slip away; the barren coastline gradually receded. Night fell and morning found us at the river mouth, where it was warm and the waves were muddy and turbid, as though we had been becalmed upon an ocean of weak tea. Round us other boats were also waiting, salt-scurfed and rust-streaked in the wintry sunlight, swinging from their heavy anchor chains, till the tide was full enough to carry them over the bar.

At mid-day the signal was given and we steamed forward. Slowly the almost invisible edge of land raised itself from the discoloured soupy water, mud flats with a vessel that had gone aground and listed in dreary abandonment like an empty tin, a factory chimney, a neat quadrangle of brick buildings, the cantonments of the English river-officials who manage its traffic and watch its tides and dangerous estuary. A strange fate for some housewife from Streatham or Ealing, this life upon the mud-flats of Taku, near the ruined forts blown up in the Boxer war. They have their children, no doubt, letters from England; their husbands drink a little and talk shop. . . .

Day by day, the steamers pass in long procession; and passengers, craning eagerly from the side, catch a first glimpse of fabulous and ancient China—railway station, flour mill, mud-built houses which accompany the windings of the stream and are clustered above ramshackle wooden piers. . . . Mud walls, roof of mud stiffened with thatch—it is the commonest form of architecture in the northern provinces. Each house is a one-storeyed yellowish cube, the colour of unbaked pottery, of the soil; every village suggests a grouping of mud pies, newly cut by some child with a sharp spade.

Lengthily we disengaged ourselves from Taku and, ship following ship at cautious intervals, steamed out across the open naked landscape. The crops had not yet begun to show, and the trees, planted closely in the fields, were shaded by a soft aura of spring buds. Nothing to hide the flatness of the plain; but near the villages, anywhere, everywhere, in the fields, beside the houses, along the river bank, family beyond family of conical mounds.

Gathered together in their congregations, some of them were big and well-kept, while others, ancient and half-obliterated, appeared to be melting into the earth. Rare was the field that had no graves; field stretched away behind field and, raked by the pallid light of the afternoon, tumulus could be seen rising behind tumulus till the prospect grew vapoury and indistinct. ·

The soil here was so thickly sown with graves that it was the dead, not the living, one was aware of first. Yet life was plentiful in the villages on either shore; soldiers, wearing uniforms of greenish khaki and the fur-eared caps which denote northern troops, drilling round a machine gun next the station; women and girls in trouser-suits of a dull red who watched us from the thresholds of their mud cottages. Men were universally dressed in blue —the dim lustreless blue of a coolie's coat or blue which had an iridescent sheen like the pollen of a South American butterfly. Blue gowns, surmounted by black calottes, strolled beside the river under the trees, ample figures, dignified and bland, smoking tasselled pipes while they took the air.

No road, which could be called a road, followed the river; but there was a rut, a dusty track, across the plain. Down it bumped a cart with a blue hood, its massive wheels grinding and squeaking as they revolved. Later, a pair of horsemen came in sight, with a string of half-wild Mongolian ponies. A single bicyclist sailed pathetically out of the distance, self-important and yet infinitely forlorn. . . . That bicyclist had the sense of covering ground, of pedalling from the past into the future. The men in the cart, the horse-dealers, the strolling pedestrians seemed to exist under the ban of an eternal present.

THE RIVER

What future could be reconciled with such a landscape
—houses and graves built of the same soil, palest tawny,
buff-coloured and ashen grey, this wide yellow stream
with low banks, washing down its silt towards the estuary? Oppressive, insignificant, but vast. If one surren-
dered one's imagination to its charm, there was a strange
beauty in the very blankness of the prospect; so harmonious were these tawny greys and yellows, so neat the scat-
tering of mud cubes that represented a village or a
homestead, so philosophic in their enormous isolation the
sedately loitering figures on the bank.

We steamed forward but the landscape did not change.
To our left there glittered through some trees the glazed
fungus-yellow roof of a small temple; and a peaked willow
pattern tower painted blue—the pale blue which marks a
stronghold of the Kuomintang—stood up for a moment
and then vanished. . . . History depends on the illusion of
time; from the endless cyclical movement of human
affairs it chooses to illuminate a small arc, and assures us
that something has happened, that progress is made. Every
country expresses its destiny through its landscape; and
in China, where distances are so huge and the extent of
recorded history so imposing, one can see the beginning
and the end of the same movement, and too much history
becomes no history at all. . . .

I am anticipating. We steamed up towards Tientsin and
our wake, as the river grew more narrow, sucked and
gurgled along the crumbling mud banks. Presently there
was a great roller sweeping behind us, a hissing wave
which brimmed up on to the fields, flooding the crops,
clawing away and tearing down big slabs of the jealously
guarded earth. This attack was repeated by successive

steamers; it happened, I suppose, with every tide. Here was a field, carefully dug and planted, in which their back-wash had channelled a slimy creek; here a house, cracked through and ready to fall, sagged over the yellow swirling water.

And then the junks. There were junks tethered from the shore, which plunged and bucked as we passed like fright-ened animals. The wave lifted them, swung them round and dragged them along, or drove them full tilt against the bank, while the boatmen, dazedly snatching up their poles, sweated and strained in the effort to keep them steady. Linked barges drifted towards us down the stream, shaggy with loads of hay to the water's edge. These, too, we set rocking and curvetting and left them behind us to slip wallowing round a bend, as we proceeded on our majestic and impartial course.

Only once were we pursued by angry voices. Along-side a large salt depository, some boatmen cursed us furi-ously as we went by, extending their open palms in ges-tures of hatred and shouting in unison with a gaggle of harsh sound. Otherwise, the people on the river bank were resigned, good-humoured, almost indifferent. They watched the foaming water claw away their fields, and laughed if a neighbour got his feet wet. Even the ducks suffered from our passage; white flotillas of them, bobbing complacently near the shore, were caught and hurled help-lessly upstream. A little boy, who was looking after them, dashed to their rescue, wading in and flourishing a stick.

The day was over when we reached the suburbs of Tientsin, and a factory whistle blew dismally from a yard. There was some shouting when a child fell into the river and was fished up, breathless and dripping, among the boats. Through the cold grim twilight which was closing down we saw the dark water-front of the modern city: villas, banks and warehouses in dark brick, a crowded quayside and a line of anchored vessels.

The steamer edged in towards the quay, and amid the Chinese crowd, densely packed beneath the rail, I noticed two Europeans standing apart. 'White Russians, probably,' said my companion, both unspeakably haggard and the worse for wear, in dirty hats, frayed collars and shapeless overcoats, gazing with pinched faces at the deck, waiting, perhaps, for somebody who never arrived. . . .

Upturned faces, shaven heads beneath the rail; then the gang-plank was dragged noisily into place. The entire crowd seemed to shove forward across the gangway and in a moment were swarming and trampling through the ship—money-changers clinking silver dollars, vague officials, soldiers and a rabble of coolies. They elbowed us; they argued fiercely over our luggage. It was snatched up and trundled off into the darkness.

The hotel entrance was a few steps across the quay. A door closed on twilight and confusion, and the smell of floor polish and a wealth of scarlet and gold paint emphasized the nationality of the proprietor. He was English; that went without saying; it was all so clean and tasteless and good-natured. The scarlet paintwork, the golden Buddhas, the assorted bric-à-brac were as English as the wicker chairs and the polished oil-cloth. One felt obliged to order immediate whiskys and sodas. English residents passed stiffly to and fro. A middle-aged woman, with a lapdog under her arm, waddled with flaccid dignity through the lounge. Two young officers, Sandhurst to the backbone, sat irreproachable and aloof in a far corner;

while the Chinese boys, like queer archangels in their white robes, slipped sulky-looking but attentive between the chairs.

Newspapers were hanging in a rack; and from these we learned that a pair of female missionaries had just been murdered in a city of the interior and that such-and-such a bandit was on the move; tens of thousands reported dead from another place—announcements which occupied as little room as a flower show in some local English sheet. Instead of a harvest festival there was a massacre, a rumoured insurrection instead of a christening. The journalists had taken their cue from the landscape; they had forgotten to appear ever so slightly surprised. . . .

Nothing matters. How different this homely cynicism from the quivering proprieties of Japanese life, by which one is encompassed as by a network of invisible threads! In China at all events one could breathe, for there was something in this squalid teeming existence, human-sized, understandable and sympathetic. It was dark now and, as I walked along the quay through the dusk, which was full of flapping ragged shapes clustered around the barrows where food was sold, and listened to the hoarse cackle of Chinese voices, I remembered the quietly shuffling Japanese crowds, their hissing courtesy and nervous self-effacement. Japanese tongues patter as monotonously as Japanese clogs; the language is alive with slippery consonants. These voices blurted and gargled, hawked and spat, in loud laughter, violent abuse or impassioned protest.

Alas, that there should be no describing smells; they give its quality to every moment of one's life, but no device of words can pin them down. A single whiff of Japan across my table would bring back to me our life there in

all its aspects more vividly than hours of writing and re-
membering. It is a faint odour, lingering and acrid; and
we had been amused some time before, in the heart of
Tokyo, on stepping over the threshold of a Chinese shop,
to feel the influence of an entirely separate world express
itself in a distinctive national fragrance which impreg-
nated the room, the shopmen and their goods.

Here it was again, and still more pungent, that fusty, in-
describable, clinging odour. As I stumbled along the
gritty, neglected quay, under the bright galleries of anchored ships, through the flapping, shadowy, spitting and
laughing crowd who gobbled their outdoor meal from
little bowls, Japan and all it stood for was mercifully distant. Back at the hotel, too, over our patriotic dinner,
with its mutton chops, watery ice, biscuits and cheese, the
contrast was brought home in another way. After the
scurrying inefficiency of Japanese servants, the portly impassive Chinese boys seemed as quick of understanding as
they were deft and noiseless, calm-moving well-disciplined
automata beside a race of self-conscious marionettes.

Next morning we caught the eleven o'clock to Peking
from the shabby desolate station across the river. There
was a great crowd on the platforms and before the book-
ing office, thin men in torn wadded or fur-lined gowns
and sleek plump persons in blue skirts and short black
coats, who possessed luggage, smoked cigarettes and read
the papers. The train itself was comfortable if rather
grimy; attendants brought us tea and steaming face towels, and for three hours we jolted on towards Peking
through a landscape nearly identical with yesterday's.

The river, it is true, was not in sight, but the ground
was as flat and carefully cultivated; everywhere, the same

families of conical graves, the same pallid soil and leafless branches. Now and then we drew up at a wayside station and hawkers swarmed with their baskets along the carriages, growing vociferous as the train began to move. They would keep step with us for a frantic hundred yards, faces distorted, feet pounding over the platform, then drop behind and lapse into an utter passivity only less remarkable than their frenzied efforts to earn a cent or two. . . .

The plain, still the plain, and some thin coppices; but we realized that we must be getting near the city. I thought of the northern approach to Rome; for this landscape somehow suggested the Roman countryside, scraps of ruin cropping out from the pale earth which had a peculiar exhausted ashy glimmer. . . . On the left, a low crenellated wall unfolded its grey ribbon across the fields. We approached and ran through under an arch, thus entering the outer city of Peking.

Peking is one of those focal points which we set ourselves as a future destination. Even at school, when the prospect of reaching Paris seemed as remote as my chances of exploring the moon, I had always meant some day to visit China, though the *how* and the *why* of it were unimaginable. Most wishes are consummated in the end; but their fulfilment is usually preceded by a decline of interest. I was no longer bent on China as years before, and the ghostly charm of gratifying a past wish, which is like sacrificing to the spirit of a remote ancestor, added a certain vividness to the present occasion. Here was Peking, these grey crenellated walls. . . . But what had become of its centre, its streets and houses? We were still, as far as I could see, in the open country; and that blue umbrella, half unfurled among the woods—pointed out to us from the carriage window as the Temple of Heaven—passed accidental and without meaning in the middle distance. Splinters of masonry, old tombs and broken gateways, appeared like edges of bone through the naked earth, and on the pale threadbare surface of the fields, grooved with dry watercourses and deep wheel-tracks, dark evergreens made blots of inky shadow.

Quite suddenly, then, the inner city came into view. We were looking down a long rutted lane, with carts, moving people and little houses, towards a two-storeyed gate-tower on the ramparts, its winged roof glistening faintly in the sun. The inner walls were much higher than the outer circuit; they marched, grey and purposeful, to left and right, shops and houses squatted flimsily beneath them. The train swung round through a wide curve and, as the storeyed gate-tower fell back, we saw a blockhouse in the angle of the wall, which resembled some gigantic military dovecote, its slanting sides chequered with black squares.

CHAPTER II

THE PALACE

We returned to Peking that same summer, and my recollections of the city and the country near are made up for the most part of double images, like two photographs superimposed on a single plate. It was early leafless spring when we first arrived; no rain had fallen since October and the cold brilliant light of the March sun lay pallid and unreal across the dust. The sky itself was a transparent crystal blue, as though the vaults of heaven were wearing thin. . . .

It was such a morning, when we disembarked on the gritty platform, and such an afternoon, when the friends with whom we stayed took us out in rickshaws to visit the Palace. The Legation Quarter adjoins the wall and the railway terminus; I see it full of feathery blossoming mimosas, growing in a twofold rank down Jade Canal Street, which shed their leaves and flowers as I fix the memory. A cool, rather bleak spring afternoon; and at the entrances of the various legations along the road, the sentries stood hugging their loaded rifles. A Chinese soldier, dressed in shabby khaki, directed the traffic at the main gate of the fortified area; while outside, on a broad stretch of open ground, men and women were cantering horses through the dust.

Yellow dust was blowing up in clouds. As the rickshaw wheels swerved and bumped across the pavement one could feel it against one's skin and in one's mouth. That gritty taste is all I remember of the journey—that and the ragged skyline of the town where it shrinks back at a respectful distance from the foreign quarter, a glimpse of mules and asses labouring by, pursued by hoarse shouts and savage whip-cracks, and the narrow lane which followed a pink wall and brought us round at last to a huge gate, tunnelled through the thickness of the ramparts, with tiers of painted gallery overhead.

Size is the canon of this architecture, height, space and solid massive dignity. If anything could dwarf these great pavilions, it is the enormous open courtyards they surround and which are strung together like a system of quadrangular lakes, white and empty among the glittering yellow roof-ridges. They seemed particularly spacious that afternoon, by that pale brilliant dusty blinding glare. We had found our way into an extensive inner courtyard, through which a deep marble-lined canal, spanned by five narrow marble bridges, describes a bow-shaped arc from side to side. Facing us, as we crossed the central bridge, was the porch of a courtyard which lay beyond, approached by a low shelf of marble steps; behind us, three pavilions looked down from a gigantic rampart substructure of pink masonry—'pink' I write for want of a better word. Pierre Loti, with melodramatic expressiveness, has described the colour as that of dried blood. In his time, no doubt, they were more vivid; they have been washed, bleached and weathered by years of neglect and are now a dull lack-lustre coral red.

The yellow roofs, too, of the pavilions and cloisters are beginning to lose their harshness with the passage of time. They are the tone of yellow lichen on a tree-trunk; while the grass, which is growing here and there unchecked between ridges of glazed tiles, makes them shimmer at every movement of the wind.... Roofs shimmered; wind blew; the courtyard was empty. An awful vacuum, seemed to exist through the whole palace. Latticed casements, in the pavilions and under the cloisters, showed black holes where the paper panes were torn. Peering in, one saw dirt and piles of rubbish. The sagging doors were roughly stamped by an official seal.

Utter emptiness as in a splendid deserted hive: and the sense of squalor which always accompanies such desertion. Something in the atmosphere of a palace or temple starts to putrefy when the human occupants vanish. And they had all gone; a lounging soldier at the gate, who wore the badge of the Nationalist government in Nanking, watched the foreign intruders with vague insolence. A spectacled person sold tickets from a box; an aged dwarf came toddling up to tear the counterfoils. ... *Sic transit*. The tag slips out so easily; there was a time when the past glories of the world went up in smoke at the touch of change. Nowadays we are more conservative of fallen splendour and empty palaces, from Peking to Madrid, are handed over to a dim rabble of custodians who punch tickets, jingle coins and erect notice boards.

Even in Peking there is some respect for 'national monuments'. True, funds meant for repairing the palace roofs are conscientiously diverted by those in office. The bright reds and blues of the painted galleries are scaling off from

A COURTYARD IN THE FORBIDDEN CITY, PEKING

the woodwork year by year; the round wooden pillars of the colonnades are gradually losing their thick coats of scarlet lacquer. . . . Still, the palace remains; it can be visited, and different sections are opened on different days, each large enough to occupy several hours, throne-rooms, audience-chambers, little gardens, an entire city, as intricate and as diverse.

After a while the effect of emptiness becomes stupefying. It would seem less empty, perhaps, if it were less impersonal, for here are none of the redeeming personal freaks, reminders of this monarch or that favourite, which are to be noticed in almost any Western palace and add to its irregularity and charm. The architecture is traditional and uncompromising; detail, often crude in colour and line, is subordinate to the spacious dignity of the plan. Only Ch'ien Lung, the great eighteenth century emperor, appears to have tampered with the rigid formalism of his dwelling. A man both powerful and unusually gifted, he went so far as to call in Western architects.

His innovation is neither conspicuous nor very large. Far away in a remote corner of the palace, he built his barbarian concubine a little bath-house, employing for this work the Jesuit missionaries who then lived on their wits at the Chinese court, in every capacity their ingenious minds suggested. . . . A tiny vaulted chamber and a paved ante-room; but in the ante-room there are two pictures on the wall, portraits of the concubine herself, painted by a Western artist in the Western manner.

Father Castiglione was his name, a versatile and sensuous Italian, an accomplished courtier—one can see that from the first picture, in which the slit-eyed Turki bedfellow of the great king is portrayed *en jardinière* upon a knoll, wearing a wide shady hat and a laced bodice, her blue over-skirt disposed around her as she reclines, holding the slender shaft of a long hoe. Clearly the artist enjoyed himself at work; this metamorphosis of Eastern slave into Western dryad must have titillated the Jesuitic sense of humour. He enjoyed, too, the delineation of a pretty woman, the pampered mistress who would have visited him among her eunuchs and sat for him under their solemn puffy guardianship, then returned to the deep seclusion of the women's quarters.

Castiglione was an Italian and a Romantic. A French painter would have been more dashing and more adept, an English artist colder but more precise. Like most Italians, he was sentimental, a 'man of feeling', and lingered with voluptuous care upon the face, its high cheekbones faintly flushed beneath the olive, the delicate smooth bridge of its short nose. His second picture, not so large and painted in oils, is less skilful and much franker in its treatment; a piece of bravado. The concubine is here portrayed with all the attributes of a classical goddess of war, a polished cuirass, a feathered helmet, a lace neck-band; she poises a marshal's baton against her thigh. The features, broad and mongol and rather sallow, have an unmistakable air of verisimilitude.

Since this portrait was preserved in the Imperial collection, one assumes that it found favour with Ch'ien Lung. What effect on that liberal and inquisitive mind, can the completed picture have had when it was shown him? In the long curious relationship of East and West, there have been few contacts more singular or more touching than the occasion recorded by these two portraits—the black-robed, soft-spoken Italian cleric, vowed to celibacy, devoted to his order, setting to work, for the greater glory of God, to fix the seductive freshness of a pagan concubine and half falling in love with his own travesty, which a breath of exotic lyricism had brought to life.

Very strange the love of God in all its forms, the apostolic impulse of the Christian church that provided the Chinese emperors for more than a century with court painters, court architects and skilled clock repairers! If the Jesuit missionaries hoped to proselytize the favourite, their calculations very soon came to nothing. She was strangled by her master's legitimate consort, as many other concubines before and since; and Ch'ien Lung, who had been called away from the capital, celebrated her loss with passionate sorrow. Castiglione lived on at the Chinese court and continued to paint pictures for the glory of God, most of them in an acquired Chinese style, so successfully that a garbled version of his name is now included in the long list of native artists. 'No Westerner could do a thing like that!' jeered a Chinese soldier, indicating a scroll, which represents an eagle beside a rivulet, the splintered rock on which the bird is perched realistically encrusted with yellow fungus, to our friend who had paused to examine it in a palace picture gallery. 'But it *is* by a foreigner . . .' he explained. The soldier would have none of his assurances. He grinned and obstinately shook his head. He knew better; of course, it was far too good.

That Castiglione, after years of patient effort, learned to paint like a second-rate Chinese journeyman, is from the Chinese point of view his greatest merit. They are contemptuous of the gardening girl in the little bathroom; and her blue overskirt and narrow eighteenth-century

bodice, her dark eyes and pearly flesh and romantic setting, do not attract many visitors to her shrine. It must be
remembered that, for most educated Chinese, the Middle
Kingdom has still a cultural monopoly. They are inclined
to think of Europe, if at all, as a purveyor of amusing
mechanical devices, clocks and motor cars and railway
engines, which may assist but cannot alter the flow of life.
It was with a clock in his hands that a Jesuit Father first
insinuated himself into the precincts of the Chinese court;
and clocks and mechanical toys and similar gew-gaws
arrived regularly as 'tribute' from the remote West and
were stored in the various apartments of the Forbidden
City.

In the Clock Pavilion we finished our afternoon. A
small crowd, Chinese of every sort, had assembled, punc-
tually on the stroke of four, to hear several dozen clocks
emit their chimes. Each is a masterpiece of Western bizar-
rerie; each has its own music, its own diversions. A young
man walked among them from case to case. He inserted a
key, turned it briskly, the dormant mechanism gave a pre-
monitory whirr; and the crystalline notes of a forgotten
tune, a jig or a gavotte or a snatch of opera, tinkled out
towards the listening Chinese. . . . This was not all; doors
flew open in the clock-case and a harlequin and other
comedians appeared to dance. Tiny figures swam slowly
across painted backgrounds; glass rods, as they revolved
side by side, gave the effect of a distant waterfall between
the trees. Elsewhere, we saw a lion-tamer and a lion; a
golden boy, in English nineteenth-century taste, with
knee-breeches and curls and a Vandyke collar, struck golden hammers jerkily on golden bells. Next to him, a little
boy, almost life-sized, wearing a gown embroidered in

petit point, touched the wires of a Louis Quinze spinet.[1]

Silvery, distinct and far-away—here and there a trifle out of tune—the ponderous splendid clocks told the hour. From case to case, the crowd wandered on; an old man whose crumpled yellow cheeks were bordered by sparse threads of frosty beard, women, middle-aged citizens, aimless soldiers, all silent, looking up and listening, with something about them ancient and yet infantile, an air of absorption which was both dignified and oddly babyish.

[1] I hope that these fascinating productions, imported at a time when Western critics were beginning to take an interest in Eastern art, may soon be more adequately described by a writer of greater scholarship than myself, to whose kindness I owe the opportunity of seeing them.

CHAPTER III

A VIEW FROM THE DAGOBA

On two sides of the enormous palace enclosure are lakes—the Chinese call them *Seas*, to indicate their magnificence and vastness—and gardens, with kiosks and covered walks, formerly the Emperor's, now 'nationalized' and thrown open. It was here that, soon after our arrival, I had my first glimpse of the Imperial breed of goldfish, which had just then been put out in wooden tubs to enjoy the mild radiance of a spring day.

The little Japanese goldfish we kept at home, their filmy divided tails and projecting eyes, were insignificant compared to these monstrous creatures which trailed or brooded in the shallow water of the tubs. As large very often as a clenched hand, gross and torpid, softly coloured and slow swimming, each of them was an Elagabalus of the fish world, a puffy boneless sybaritic freak, accompanied when it moved by its own draperies, a tail and fins considerably longer than itself, which eddied, rippled and drooped like a gauzy train. Their eyes bulged vacuous from their heads; their stomachs were stretched so tightly as to be almost spherical. Some were a slippery silver-gilt, others a piebald red and silver. There were fish with warty scarlet crests, imitating the wattles of a turkey's throat, fishes in a lustreless leaf-brown and fishes in dead and sooty black.

Those last were particularly splendid. Imagine a group of opulent French *bourgeoises*, inconsolable yet voluptuous in widow's weeds. They suggested the catafalque or the *crime passionel*, the husband-slayer sobbing in the dock or the Niobe-like relict of a great man oozing between the arms of her supporters. They seemed to swim to the measures of the Dead March, and their scales, that soft and sooty black, were unrelieved by the least metallic shine. They did not swim, so much as drift, about the tub, and usually hung immobile near the surface, or reposed limp and large upon the bottom, their fleshy jaws quietly opening and shutting. Many centuries of cultivation lay behind them, the Bourbons or the Hapsburgs of their breed, a queer comment on nature's elasticity and the Chinese passion for stretching it to the full and squeezing a strange beauty from horror and ugliness.

Just when this passion for the grotesque, for shapes bulbous, writhen and twisted, gnarled and bent, first made its appearance in the Chinese world I must leave it to other writers to determine. No doubt the spread of Lamaistic Buddhism, introduced from the North by barbarian emperors, refined on an inbred predeliction. The later Chinese emperors were all lamaists; and the imperial park in which the goldfish are to be seen centres round a monument of that cult, a *dagoba* or bottle-shaped stucco cone, that shines from far away over the city and is approached by a marble bridge across a lotus lake.

Again, two photographs present themselves—the round arches of the broad marble bridge reflected upon the

smoothly rippling moat which also mirrors the squat pin-
nacle and its wooded eminence; and the same moat so
crowded with pink lotus blossoms that no reflection could
find a place among their leaves. They do not rest upon the
surface like Japanese water-lilies; but every blossom and
every pointed roseate bud is carried high into the air by a
green stem—straight and thick—as are the circular flat
leaves which a fall of rain sprinkles with big moonstones.

How justly chosen as the flowers of Paradise! Many
flowers have a wanton wilful delicacy, evasive and insubstantial, like a teasing perfume. The pink lotus is as unmistakable as a pretty face, its green stem shooting up-
wards from the water and its silky petals opening and falling away, leaving behind a green seed-pod which resembles a pepper pot. . . . Righteous souls are reborn on an
extended lotus cup; while the less righteous must content
themselves with a closed bud, a gigantic pink pavilion
throughout eternity. They cannot see the splendid visions
of Paradise; a fancy which has inspired a Japanese poet to
compare fugitive lovers in a palanquin to a pair of spirits
who inhabit the same flower. . . .

For some reason the paths leading to the Dagoba are
haunted by men who offer one picture postcards which
grow progressively more indecent with each refusal. They
follow one to the top of the last flight, apathetic yet persistent like summer blowflies, then silently drop off and
disappear. A marble platform stands at the foot of the
white cone and, leading from it, under a circular tiled roof,
is a deep niche protected by a grill, enclosing a hideous
polychrome demon presence which flourishes more arms
than one can count and snarls horribly with as many clustered heads. The creations of the lamaistic cult have a

loathsomeness transcending all absurdity. They seem, as do the Aztec gods and goddesses, to have sunk their roots deep in blood and squalor, till their meanest manifestations are genuinely horrible. They have an obscenity much profounder than the merely phallic; and it was difficult to look at this tawdry demon, fresh painted and in excellent repair, without a movement of disgust and even alarm.

He seemed ill-suited to the landscape at his feet—to what one knows of the faiths which it has matured, the nihilistic abstractions of Zen Buddhism, the woolly but hard-wearing Confucian precepts. . . . Beneath this terrace, on a spring afternoon, the grey latticework of tree-tops, which covered the hillside, was beginning to flush dimly with green buds; while 'kingfisher' roofs, blue and yellow, still shone up through a canopy of naked branches from pavilions lower down the sharp ascent. To the left, the ochreous tiles of the Imperial Palace made a solid quadrangular glittering mass; and the city wall, and the gate-towers which rose above it, faintly rimmed the level expanse of Chinese houses.

Grey, a pale ashen grey, predominated—the grey of naked boughs beginning to bud, a long grey arm of misty-looking water, which extended, dull and smooth, beside the palace. A dull firmament, cold and lofty overhead, was speckled dark with the passage of migrating ducks, thousands of them, travelling very high, northwards, in broken strings and wedges.

During the warm months, Peking is a forest city. As one looks down from the platform of the Dagoba, beyond the palace roofs which quiver fiercely in the sun, the houses seem to have lost themselves amid the trees, only the distant ridge of the city ramparts separating the trees within from the trees without, the narrow streets from the flowering shady fields where the ripening crops are sometimes taller than a man.

Behind the Dagoba is a labyrinth of rockeries, winding paths, grottos, nooks and corners, all designed with wanton picturesqueness but nowadays full of dust and drifted leaves. My memory of it belongs to the earlier season and has the chill light of a declining afternoon. It was very cold, and, on our way home through the streets, we met a company of dejected youthful soldiers, many of them boys in their middle teens, who straggled by to unconvincing military music. Somewhere the great war-game was being played, combinations of militarists were being schemed. Not far from the new capital itself, a discontented 'war lord' bestrode the line, threatening the helpless central government with a descent in embattled might upon its treasury. . . .

At least, that was the rumour in Peking; and Peking, though it is no longer the seat of government, echoes to every scrap of political gossip. So-and-So, you may be casually informed, is sending 'eight picked Soochow virgins' in order to strengthen his alliance with the Young Marshal whose exacting taste in concubines is well known. Marshal Chang, one was told during the summer, thought of founding an empire in the North. True, his father, the redoubtable Old Marshal, blown up with the connivance of the Japanese, had begun life as a bandit in Manchuria. *Cela n'empêche pas.* . . . Many former Chinese dynasties have owed their origin to the political sense of an ex-bandit, in a country where bandits and soldiers are much alike and to-day's national champion is yesterday's brigand.

CHINOISERIE: A SOUTHERN CHINESE GARDEN

Young Chang—he is approaching middle age, though he still exists on his reputation for dashing youthfulness— was strongly favoured by the gossips at that time. China needed an Emperor, they said. . . . They said it, not passionately, dogmatically, as one would have heard it said, for example, by a French monarchist, but with a quiet good-natured shrug and smile. It might have been a chess problem they were discussing, so bland and even-tempered were their voices, Mr. A the rather sad-faced Manchu gentleman and his friend Mr. B the distinguished actor—a game, a little problem of family life, as who should say it wouldn't be a bad thing if his parents sent young Smith out to the colonies, or if old Nobodaddy were elected to the Parish Council. . . .

Parochial—perhaps that is the right word. I had already noticed how China at its most horrific has a homeliness which is reflected by the foreign papers; and, in the gossip which sometimes came our way, there was always the same note of quiet provincialism. Any attempt to find a clue through Chinese politics seemed to lead direct into a small and airless room, crowded with the members of a single family. Take the genesis of the government at Nanking. Dr. Sun Yat-sen, my informant would explain, had a concubine, and that concubine had a brother. . . . But recent history is a warren of such rooms, the occupants of this room plotting against the occupants of that; while trap doors and secret passages and hidden stairs wind up and down and to and fro. Strange whispers are wafted into the open; solemn-looking gentlemen shake their heads. And the representatives of the imperialistic Western powers, secluded in their comfortable Legation Quarter, play a part which grows more and more ineffectual.

Events, which are utterly mysterious when considered from the Western point of view—the point of view which insists on presupposing that politicians necessarily have policies and that even an ex-bandit may be a patriot—become simple as elucidated by a Chinese. Somebody or other has a nephew and somebody else is heavily in debt to him. *Ergo.* . . . A smile unweaves the mystery. It is just a big problem of family life, the politics of an overcrowded tenement, if you imagine the tenement as co-existing with, or being raised on the foundations of, a huge necropolis.

For in China the world beyond the grave exercises an influence which is not merely psychological. A large and growing city at the present day, anxious to extend its ancient boundaries, is apt to find its progress held up by a ring of graveyards which it dare not break open. Death, at any rate in Northern Europe, has been robbed in recent years of half his panoply:

'Death, be not proud, though some have calléd thee
Mighty and dreadful, for thou art not so. . . .'

exclaims with Donne the modern sanitary inspector. Gravestones may glimmer like false teeth; but one seldom meets death upon the breeze. In Peking, on the other hand, during the warm months, as one drives out of the city into the country, one passes through successive zones of death, where death, so to speak, jumps up on to the running-board of the car and one holds one's handkerchief firmly across one's nose—which would be sufferable, did the generations of dead men confine their influence to a sudden bad smell.

Unfortunately, their influence is more pervasive. Death confers a prestige in the Far East with which no efforts of

the living can compare. Reformers, who were revolutionary during their lifetime, become aristocrats in the hierarchy of the dead. Confucius may be slowly losing ground,
but Dr. Sun is stepping into his niche. It has long been a
custom in the East to absorb the beneficent properties of
holy writ by the easiest and most obvious method, in
other words, by masticating and digesting them; and,
though Chinese and Japanese intellectuals may have given
up swallowing a text whole or applying it to the skin by
way of cataplasm, one is frequently aware of a disposition
to do the same thing through the eyes, to 'swallow a text
whole' in another sense. Hence the continued renown of
Dr. Sun and of the book in which his gospel is set forth—
a work of which the intention is as enlightened as the
reasoning is ingenuously obscure.

But my business is primarily with things seen, and the
foregoing fragmentary generalizations are only relevant
should they help to supply a background. First suggested
by the memory of marching soldiers, peasant boys in their
shabby khaki uniforms trailing off down a cold and dusty
thoroughfare, let them recede with the noise of trampling
feet, sharp words of command and brassy music. Soldiers
are not important in the end, generals a mere accident of
nature, like smallpox and floods and other scourges. '*Il
faut cultiver notre jardin*' still holds good, though all the
generals in the world are about their ears.

CHAPTER IV

A DINNER PARTY

Into the cultivation of this garden, such as it is, goes an odd mixture of slovenliness and diligence. Broad streets intersect the quadrangular city, long stretches of small delapidated shops, many of them with worm-eaten carved faces and the toppling poles which were once a sign of Imperial patronage—restaurants, second-hand shops, numerous clock repairers. Inside, there is a strong musty smell, and several persons, sometimes indifferent and sometimes friendly, stir and look up as the door opens. An old man sits in a corner smoking his pipe. Very often, if one has not visited the shop before, they signify that one's custom is not needed. 'There isn't any!' they retort doggedly to each question. The old man, straight wisps of silver hair descending from a yellow wrinkled upper lip, continues to suck the mouthpiece of his pipe, prepared to outlast the tiresome visitors as he has outlasted so much else, good and bad.

One leaves again; and, if it is early in the year, clouds of dust may be chasing along the street, or a dust-storm, moving very high, blown eastwards by the strong desert-wind, may diffuse an unearthly mustard-coloured light,

as lurid as the thick gloom of a London fog. Rickshaws
pass; in blue jackets and blue drawers, the rickshaw coolies pad between the shafts, turning to shout hoarsely at
another coolie who has swerved in without warning across
the road.

The hoarse voices and gargling oaths of quarrelsome
rickshaw men must not be forgotten in a description of
Peking street life. Two coolies stand yelling face to face;
and, though the argument concerns a single copper coin,
jaws work and eyes flash with intense hatred. They push,
grapple and spit and are pulled apart. They separate, still
turning to shout an insult, and lurch away, muttering
fiercely to themselves.

Profanity is eloquent in Peking. It has always seemed a
grave reflection on the Japanese character, that their
language, with the exception of the word 'fool'—and
'countryfied fool' is extremely strong— should contain no
opportunities for invective. I was satisfied, however, in
Peking. Sisters, old grandmothers and other connections
are tersely passed judgment on in current oaths or recommended as proper objects for nameless profligacy. 'F——
your sister!' scolds one coolie to the next; and this advice
is so far from being obscene that an acquaintance tells of
hearing a respectable man playfully hush his infant to its
rhythm, just as a Cockney, while dandling his child, might
refer to it with real tenderness as 'You little b——'.

Besides the thudding feet and hoarse throats of the rickshaw coolies, Peking, especially in the warm weather, re-
sounds to the whining hubs of countless water-carts,
wooden barrows, cumbersome and heavy, of which the
single wheels squeak fearfully through the back streets,
while their precious water puddles the white dust. And,

now and then, one catches the sound of lama trumpets, the curved metal tubes of a distant procession which bray and boom, resonant yet soft, like the voice of an enormous rutting stag or the complaint of a minotaur in love, amid the narrow streets around the Lama Temple.

I see these Peking vistas in different aspects; the horned roof of a gate tower in the haze, concluding a long perspective of lighted shops, as it looms through the violet fog of a dusty evening; and the same roof, its glittering green ridges, sagging, broken-backed and tufted with grass, mercilessly displayed by the spring sun which fills the dishevelled street with warmth and gaiety. The days were often warm, but the nights were arctic; the night skies of March and early April were frigid as a vaulting of black glass, where big stars sparked and trembled in hungry brilliance. Very pleasant then to ride swiftly through the streets; but the rickshaw men, waiting outside a cinema, coughed and shivered beneath thin jackets and torn gowns, waking up when the close of the performance released a crowd and the last fares of the evening came in sight.

Babel, a hopeless scrimmage around the doors, shouts and clashing spokes and furious curses. Chinese policemen, brandishing leather straps, hit right and left to clear the way. No nonsense in Peking about human equality; though it may be doubted whether the liability to be beaten, and the opportunity to beat oneself if one gets a chance, is not in essence more subtly democratic—since it hints that the mere possession of a strap is ultimately the only real and lasting difference—than the suaver methods which are employed in Western countries.

At this hour the broad pavements of the Ginza would

be populous with the usual evening throng, shuffling endlessly to and fro before the night-stalls, self-important,
subdued and well-conducted. Yet under the even flow of
Japanese life one reaches down to a fundamental lack of
sympathy; and in China, for all its desolation, are still
traces of a world one can comprehend. Deep intimacy, of
course, one does not expect; but the small change of
ordinary social existence circulates between Chinese
and Western barbarian with a facility undreamt of in
Japan.

There is a certain engaging cynicism about the Chinese;
and this, too, helps to smooth the path of friendship.
Neither Mr. A nor Mr. B—the Manchu gentleman and the
successful actor—showed any signs of that paralysing
diffidence, shot through as it often is by a half-sneer,
which makes the hospitality of most Japanese such heavy
going. They had none of that uncomfortable defensive-
ness; they did not apologize for China or their own homes.
When they invited us to dine with them among their families, they played the host with a well-bred lack of embarrassment.

I remember best Mr. B's dinner party. It took place
during July on a sultry evening, and, after picking up Mr.
and Mrs. A, we set out in a car to find the house, which
was hidden in the narrow streets of a remote quarter. Mr.
B was affluent for a Chinese; but the blind wall and low
gateway were unpretentious. A servant with a lantern
came to the door, and we were led past the traditional
screen of masonry, which shut off a direct view from the
street, first into one tiny courtyard and then a second,
where Mr. B appeared vaguely from the dusk, clad in a
crumpled suit of silk pyjamas.

'Mr. B does the cooking,' explained his friend; he was pleased to see us but looked bemused and a little sleepy. Would we wait? . . . There were some other people coming. This way. And we passed through into a larger courtyard and over the threshold of a pavilion at the end, a single high-roofed room with paper windows, furnished in the modern Chinese taste.

Black-wood chairs, a long marble-topped dining table strewn casually with cups and porcelain spoons; behind a screen an opium-smoking couch which took the form of a huge brassy Western bed. So much for the solid equipment of the place; its knick-knacks were multitudinous and strangely assorted—photographs and postcards on the wall, fretwork brackets, cheap ash trays, tin alarum clocks, little vases which suggested the trophies of an English fair ground, and a big oil painting of our host's lamented father in the robe, cap and button of a mandarin.

His mother was still alive and about the house, a grim-looking but amiable old woman, one eyeball filmy white with cataract, its companion keen and malicious in a wrinkled face. How old were we? Her inquisitiveness was unabashed, and she laughed and nodded shrewdly at our replies. Her son flitted away towards the kitchen. We drank tea and waited for the other guests.

There were many flies in the lofty stone-paved room and, as servants and untidy children from the yard wandered through to set dishes on the table, they swung down with languid interest about the food, sometimes driven off but always returning. Dinner and the rest of the party were equally behindhand; but at last, cheerfully apologizing for the delay, a plump young man dressed in a silk cassock and his slender painted wife were introduced.

Accustomed as we were to Japanese women, their squabby figures and the unconquerable shyness, from which they occasionally emerged with a faint giggle like fish momentarily rising from a deep pool, Chinese ladies seemed elegant and self-assured. Mrs. A, for example, was a Manchu and, though not yet twenty, a perfect woman of the world. She was plain but had humour and determination, which were expressed in every movement that she made, the toss of her straight fringe over her forehead and a bold easy way of crooking her legs, that showed wrinkled cotton stockings and cambric drawers, descending half an inch below the knee.

The new arrival was prettier and more self-conscious; she, too, was very young but looked determined. A tight tubular dress, discreetly flowered, with a high stiffened collar at the neck, sheathed her youthful flattish body from chin to ankle. Under its hem appeared heelless satin slippers; she wore rouge, a single blossom, several bracelets, and was obviously much preoccupied by the foreign visitors, often catching our eyes during the meal and letting them go again with a faint malicious smirk, like a child who enjoys *pinging* a strand of elastic.

The two husbands seemed to suffer their wives gladly, Mr. A from what I heard on another occasion being kept under control with special thoroughness. It was even said—a statement I cannot vouch for—that to please his wife he had put down both his concubines, but that she herself continued to smoke opium, on the grounds that it helped to reduce her figure. . . . Mr. A did not follow his wife's lead, for reasons which were hygienic rather than moral. Smoking, he had confided to our friend, was conducive in the long run to sexual impotence, and personally he thought the sacrifice too great. A good-natured, un-embittered man. His father, in the old Manchu days, had been the governor of an important northern province, and Mr. A belonged to the great fellowship, as widespread in modern China as in the modern West, of impoverished and humbled patrician stragglers who warm their hands round the camp fires of art.

But Mr. B's dirty children and bad food were, I think, not entirely to his liking. Pekingese cooking is often delicious; golden duck-skin, the white marrow of the duck's spine and duck's liver, prepared with different sauces, can all be recommended to the Western gourmet. Mr. B, alas, was a poor cook and the meal, through which we slowly worked our way, was one of the least appetizing I have ever eaten. I remember trying mincemeat wrapped in lotus leaves. We unrolled the greasy coverings with our fingers and deposited them round our plates on the swimming table-top. Alternatively, they could be cast on to the floor which served as spitoon and general rubbish heap.

The meal was over, and kindly Mr. A enquired if it was true I wanted to smoke. Mr. B, he said, was a great smoker; and two pipes and a large variety of implements had been laid out on a tray ready for use. Were opium-smoking common in Japan, it would be explained by Japanese, to whom one mentioned it, as a fast-vanishing relic of mediævalism, irrelevant to the 'progressive' tendency of modern life. Opium? A furious smile would be the answer; whereas the obliging and good-humoured Mr. A conducted me without embarrassment behind the screen. I was to stretch myself on the cushions of the brass bedstead, while he set to work preparing the pipes.

Opium smoking is the staidest form of indulgence, the

most sedentary and least uncivilized of all the vices. First the raw opium in its pot, dark viscous stuff which can be bought for a few dollars, must be collected with an adroit twist around a pin; next, it must be cooked over the lamp, slowly twirled with soft bubbling and crackling noises, till it has hardened and can be applied to the bowl of the pipe, where it is wreathed about a tiny central aperture. Then the pipe-bowl is turned down towards the flame. . . . 'Imagine,' said Mr. A, as he finished his work, 'you are a child that sucks its mother's breast.' With this disconcertingly Freudian piece of advice, he put the polished tube into my hands, explaining how I should recline near the lamp and draw regularly on the large silver mouthpiece, regularly exhaling clouds of smoke, never allowing the bowl to leave the flame and never pausing, or it would immediately go out; which, at a first essay, it incontinently did. . . .

'Try again.' He carefully repaired the damage and pierced a fresh hole through the cooked opium. After that, an observant psycho-analyst would have been satisfied by my progress in the art. Fifteen, perhaps twenty, puffs all told; and the strong pleasant odour of the drug had begun to drift in heavy wreaths across the room. How to describe its curious fragrance? Wholesome and reassuring as the scent of a hayfield, with which, indeed, I thought I detected a distant affinity. There was nothing 'exotic' about the odour; it had the innocence and heady perfume of the vegetable world.

And the effects? Our friends had been amused by the naive hankering I had evinced for odd sensations. The total result of a few pipes was mildly sedative; one lay back acquiescent and at peace—a result in which the ritual of smoking, the deep regular inhalations which it demands and the soft glow of the lamp on the smoker's face, were no doubt a contributory cause. Ill-effects there were none but a slight giddiness. To become an addict, one must smoke industriously for many months; and opium, in spite of its awful legend, during the experimental stage is not habit-forming.

The pipes and the bed were Mr. B's, and, once I had satisfied a tourist's curiosity, he took my place with some relief upon the cushions. In the meantime, a concert was being arranged; Mr. A had taken out his violin and, with cocked ear, was tuning it across his knee. The plump young man, who had kept us waiting for dinner, had also brought his violin under his arm. His wife, though she protested she was not in voice, was pushed into the centre of the floor.

Then, suddenly, the accompaniment burst out. Each fiddle consisted of a round case, much the size and form of a bisected gourd, with a membrane stretched taut over the open end. Fiddle sticks, threaded through the strings, were sawed at eccentric angles to and fro, the fiddle case resting on the performer's knee and held upright there by his left hand upon the neck. The music they produced was severely classical; it reached us from so shadowy a past that the dim strains of the most recondite English lutanists were by comparison as the comic songs of yesterday. Who knows what semi-mythical Han emperor had voiced his sorrow through these despairing reedy sounds that wailed and fretted, gnashed and thrilled, soared and broke, with the jagged intermittency of a nervous seismograph? Dirge, love song, chant of triumph—it was all one. But here the singer, who had been standing among the chairs, coyly twisting her graceful hands against her stomach in the attitude of an embarrassed Western school-girl, gave vent to an anguished nasal cry. She had half turned her back upon the audience and sang looking up towards the roof, like a child asked to 'oblige' at a village concert. Now and then I caught glimpses of her profile, her straight fringe and a row of pretty teeth which shone white between contracted scarlet borders.

She paid no attention to the violinists, and the violinists paid no attention to one another. They sat humped over their fiddles with weaving elbows, and all around the wall and in the doorway admiring children and domestics paused to listen. Greasy dishes still heaped the marble table-top; and I remember noticing on a console at the side two gaudy beribboned English chocolate boxes, quite empty but preserved in the same spirit as makes Western families collect coloured Chinese tea chests. A poignant not easily forgotten scene. Here were Mr. A and his companion, each fiddling with magnificent independence, their fiddle bows rasping and whining across the strings; and here the *diva*, her linked hands upon her stomach, jigging absently from her left foot to her right, produced a thin plangent feline wail, high as the faint squeak of a hunting bat, but drawn out through agonising modulations till we began to shift uneasily in our chairs.

From where I was sitting near the screen I had also a view of the brass bedstead and of Mr. B's face upon the cushions, picked out by the warm glow of the little lamp: his straggling chin-tuft of black and wiry beard, his wrinkled forehead and hollow sucking cheeks. His eyes were almost shut and he looked happy; except to prepare another pipe—which he accomplished with quick automatic gestures—he did not shift from his position on the mattress; and, though his ostensible motive in retiring had been to strengthen his nerves and sweeten his voice, it was soon plain that only under compulsion was there any likelihood of his ever getting up.

Ten—eleven pipes; but I lost count. The music had abruptly rasped to a pause, and we asked if Mr. B wouldn't sing, for it was Mr. B we had originally come to hear. Mr. A went over and touched his arm; he opened his eyes and ran his fingers through his locks, pulling them down desperately on to his brow. Yes, with pleasure. . . . Then he rolled off the bed and staggered into the centre of the room, hair wild and his silk pyjama suit, which was dishevelled as if he slept in it beneath a haystack, gaping to show a strip of sallow skin. Dazedly he kept rumpling his hair. The drum! He would play upon the kettle-drum. It was dragged forward, but the tympanum was too slack, and Mr. B seized a trailing sheet of newspaper, held a match to it and waved it recklessly to and fro, thus warming up the surface of the torpid instrument and broadcasting large fragments of fiery paper and big drifting feathers of black ash in a Pompeian whirl of smuts throughout the room.

His performance itself was an anti-climax. Many negro bandsmen in night-club orchestras have greater skill with the drum than Mr. B. Sleepily he thumped and twanged on the limp surface, and hoarsely, in the bird-utterance of a Chinese actor, he sent his voice to explore the limits of high cacophony. Then he stopped, and stood smiling and slightly swaying. . . . We said good-bye. He retired behind the screen.

CHAPTER V

IN THE COUNTRY

A single occasion; but I have chosen to describe it because it shines with an especially distinct lustre. It seems typical somehow, as I look back, of our memories of Peking and the Chinese, long broken-fronted dusty Chinese streets and plump-sedate or ragged-obstreperous passers-by, empty palaces and winged towers falling to ruin. . . .

Beyond the walls, you are at once in the open country, and far ahead over a grey expanse of fields—deep luxuriant green during the summer—stretches a fragile and lovely line of rambling hilltops, the Western Hills with the Summer Palace at their feet and many temples half hidden among their folds. It is here you drive out in the warm months. There are few roads in the vicinity of Peking—few, at least, that an English motorist would acknowledge—and the car struggles and bumps down a shallow water-course or jolts along a pitted and ruined track, made rougher by huge irregularly jointed flagstones.

In the summer, you meet strings of desert camels. These dark brown thick-coated solemn beasts are driven in from the remote regions in which they herd, and carry sacks of

197

coal and even sandwich-boards. They are too stupid to be much frightened by the car and pass with that sibilant wheezing and snorting which is peculiar to camels all over the world. Their peaked humps sag and sway at every stride, and behind them their long-legged and woolly calves, already wearing an expression of imbecile arrogance, hold up their thin scrawny birdlike necks.

Sometimes a procession fills the road. It was an April morning, and we had just left the city gate, on our way to a hot spring in the country where there is a restaurant, a bath-house and a little park. Our road was a hollow track between fields, and through the haggard diffused glare of a sudden dust-storm shadowy figures wavered ahead in a long line. First antiquated pillbox carriages, jolting and bumping, which contained silent personages dressed in white; then a litter, a sort of crazy palanquin, which lurched forward on the shoulders of ragged coolies who wore green and red coats and black hats, each hat with a broken bedraggled feather. A funeral; the red-domed palanquin sheltered the wooden coffin of the deceased, who had evidently been respectable and well-to-do. Perhaps thirty men puffed and sweated under its shafts; and as many more, with no visible occupation, kept them company in straggling array. Some, red-coated, bore wands of white paper; next a paper horse and cart and a paper servant—the servant had a grey trilby on his head—were carried along, to be burnt during the ceremony, as an economical substitute for a genuine holocaust. Mythological animals of moss and wicker—birds and lions were chiefly represented—came tagging after a paper sedan chair, empty but adorned by a large wreath.

There was much else; I have forgotten the other accessories, and what I remember is a strange and tattered frieze, slipshod and phantasmal amid the dust which blew in a gritty hurricane across the road and gave the ragged coats and soiled plumes of the swarming bearers, the lurching bulk of the enormous palanquin, a ghostly vagueness appropriate to the occasion, as though the dead man had already begun on earth his journey through the twilight of the nether world.

Our car hooted impatiently in the rear, then inch by inch pushed its way towards the front. No one appeared to resent this interruption: mourners and bearers were chatting and joking among themselves, spitting and breaking step and falling out. There was no dignity, no attempt at perfect drilling; it was as informal and inconsequent as a dream and, for that reason, maybe, the more impressive. The great processions of the Middle Ages were like that, and even to-day the solemnities of the Roman Church are enacted with the same disregard for detail. . . .

The cortège seemed endless as we edged by; but, at last, we were clear of it on the open road. We bathed that morning in deliciously warm water which bubbles up into covered cement cisterns, and ate a meal, very good and very large, among other dishes some dark green ancient eggs, tasting of the scum on a mantled pond. After lunch we had meant to walk across the park; but there was a soldier with a fixed bayonet at the gate and a surly official, in a pay-box, who demanded an entrance fee. The local general, explained a waiter at the hotel, had decided to collect an arbitrary 'squeeze'; so we turned away and set off into the country, making for a rocky bluff above a village.

On the hilltop was an edifice that suggested a fort. We climbed up and saw that it was a temple. A square of buildings surrounded a small yard, and at the back, under a dilapidated penthouse, sat a placid family party of crumbling gods with smooth egg-shaped faces and affectionate smiles. Rubbish heaped the altar around their feet, and the roof was falling down upon their heads. There were many names scratched largely over the plaster and, though some incense sticks had recently been set burning and their fine heavy ash spattered the floor, the whole place smelt of mildew and decay.

Behind the temple was a narrow grassy platform, fringing a precipice which dropped sheer into the plain. A tranquil, rather misty afternoon; beneath us, the tawny-pallid earth, tilled minutely as far as the eye could reach, so that it resembled the ribbed texture of a coarse fabric, rolled off towards a distant line of hills, towards another village set about with smoky trees, islanded in the huge monotony of furrowed soil. A hazy golden light suffused the landscape and its mountainous edge, across the sweep of hollow plain, was barely indicated, like the background of a Sung picture. Faint paths strayed diagonally through the fields, reminding me of the seams in a piece of cloth; and whitish smears—streaks of salt or lime—resembled a discoloration in the weave.

Two wagons were moving along a path, and further away there were some packhorses upon a trail. Seen from above, they progressed with painful slowness, little carts dragging and bumping towards the horizon, sending up to us the sharp whine of their wooden hubs, no objective in sight before the village, and that many miles still to go. Hubs squeaking, a whip cracking, dogs barking. A pair of large curly-tailed dogs raced in a broad ellipse over the fields, making tracks of white dust as they revolved. Another cart, moving in the opposite direction, met and passed the two carts I had first noticed.

Our point of view was Olympian from the hilltop; and here, if this book were written in French, some magniloquent commonplace might be introduced—for the edification of a hypothetical reader, himself sensitive to the charm of lonely landscapes, the air of utter tedium they exhale, as haunting as the long story of an obscure life. Commonplace, certainly, were the emotions it aroused; but then commonplace emotions are sometimes the strongest, if only because we are obliged to enjoy them in secret. I pretended to be unaffected by what we saw, and tried to remember some verses I had once read, a fragment of a seventeenth-century poem—perhaps Joseph Beaumont's laborious arid *Psyche*, though I have never yet traced them to their source:

'Huge plains and lowly cottages forlorn,
    Rounded about by the vast wavering sky. . . .'

I thought that they epitomized the present scene; but my companion, when I repeated them for his benefit, said doubtfully that he did not think them very good. I said that I thought 'wavering' was expressive. . . . We both got up and started to walk down the hill.

As we climbed down, Peking was straight in front and the Summer Palace away upon the right, under a final spur of the Western Hills. To the Summer Palace we had driven some days before. Its lake is beautiful; but the pavilions and covered walks, built about the middle of the last century, bear horrid witness to the depravity of

Chinese taste. They are arranged with a certain magnificence upon the hillside, with a sense of symmetry that stresses and underlines their tawdry unimaginative detail. Chinese architecture, at its latest and most vulgar, has a very close resemblance to Western counterfeits; and, walking through the courtyards of the Summer Palace, one might have been visiting some gimcrack Chinese fantasy, conceived by the promoters of a World Fair and now relegated to the dreary seclusion of a public park.

It was obvious, as one entered the great pavilions, that the Empress Dowager's personal taste in bric-à-brac must have coincided, to an extraordinary degree, with that of the least enlightened English tourists. Screens with grisly inlay of mother-of-pearl, vases of monstrous shape and hue, frightful bronzes, worthless pictures and tortured lacquer work made an ensemble which would have disgraced a Victorian drawing-room. Blackwood chairs framed slabs of streaky marble. There were many clocks, one in the form of a lighthouse. A row of gilt seats, upholstered in yellow satin, evoked the gas-lit routs of the Second Empire.

We left the Summer Palace without regret. Another palace—all that now remains of it—lies some distance across the fields from the main road. Here stood the original Summer Palace; but Lord Elgin and the allied French commander, exasperated, not inexcusably, by the Chinese who had taken and tortured a pacific British envoy, and otherwise shown their contempt for Western barbarism, pillaged and burnt it as an inducement to better manners. This happened in the less self-conscious 'sixties; and it is fair to add that the savagery of the foreign troops was more sparing than the rapacity of the Chinese. Till the

early years of the twentieth century, I am told, the buildings we hoped to visit were largely intact. Since then a
succession of Chinese generals have used the ruins as a
quarry for cut stone.

Even the site on which it rose is now obscure. There
were some poor-looking mud cottages in a field, and a
little boy came out to show us the way; a long walk over
rough and tussocky ground, interrupted by a chain of
muddy pools, almost empty and thickly grown with
spectral reeds. Here was a lake, or what must once have
been a lake, enclosing an islet where a pavilion must have
stood. Beyond lay a shapeless pile of masonry—all that is
left of the rococo garden-houses, designed by the Jesuits
for Ch'ien Lung.

Among the other ingenious labours which they accomplished, the Jesuits constructed for their Imperial patron a
whole quarter of his palace in Western style. This elegant
addition seems to have been used as a repository of European toys. Lord Macartney, ambassador to the Chinese
court, despatched by the government of George III,
stayed here in great discomfort for some time, but does
not mention having seen any Western buildings. True, he
was not allowed to move about, and one imagines that in
the enormous palace enclosure, a labyrinth of water-ways
and small pavilions, only threaded by mandarins and
privileged eunuchs, the Jesuits' work was as insignificant
and easy to miss as some Oriental 'folly' in a Western
garden.

Charming it must have been, when it was new; for,
though one is disappointed at a first glance which reveals
a chaotic mass of fallen stone, with some patience and a
little imagination the main outline of various buildings

can be restored. Fountains made a large part of the plan. Ch'ien Lung had been greatly interested, the story goes, by a fountain he had seen portrayed in a Western picture. He asked Castiglione to explain it and, much delighted by what was told him of its use, expressed the desire to have a fountain of his own. The Jesuits immediately complied; their fountain was improved on by a small pavilion. Presently fountains, topiary work and an elaborate maze had grown up under the supervision of le père Benoit, whose masterpiece was a kind of aquatic clock, effigies of the Hours, animal-headed, taking turns in jetting out streams of water.

It was on to the ruins of this building that we first stumbled. Beneath a terrace, which once supported a pavilion, there was yet to be seen a beautifully moulded scallop shell. Hence the water must have spouted in a broad sheet, parting and rippling musically away down channels which extended on either side, again converging through many decorative involutions. Under the shell had been a grotto in *rocaille*, and a triangular strip of pond, dividing the Hours, which squatted, six by six, on opposite banks.

The pavilions were roofed with glittering Chinese tiles, and bright shards, yellow and green, lay underfoot. There were statues—only the pedestals now remained. The whole effect must have been of fairy-tale extravagance, brilliant, impromptu, a trifle sketchy—a splendid 'surprise' got up for the jaded Emperor, as parents arrange treats for a difficult child. Inside was his collection of Western objects, Venetian mirrors—Ch'ien Lung had so many of them that he could afford to cut them up to furnish window panes—French furniture, Gobelins and jewelled

OUTER GATEWAY:
TEMPLE OF HEAVEN, PEKING

A GATEWAY:
TEMPLE OF HEAVEN, PEKING

clocks. When the foreign troops arrived, they were still in place, although damaged by neglect and careless handling. The fountains, too, fell rapidly into disrepair; and after a time the eunuchs deputed to guard them employed coolies to fetch water for the cascades. The Emperor's exotic plaything was already broken, when it perished at the hands of Western soldiery.

First the eunuchs, then the foreigners and local 'war lords'. A few columns and scraps of archway still remain, heavily laden with somewhat gross and showy ornament. Melancholy is the impression they make to-day. No sea-beast, washed up on an alien shore or left to languish in a dismal aquarium tank, ever looked so helplessly out of its element as these ruins in the desolate Chinese plain. Rice fields, slimy ditches, withered grass; here and there peasant labourers in blue cotton, chopping with clumsy mattocks at the soil. Over the treetops peered the stump of an ancient pagoda, itself neglected and ready to fall. . . .

Ruins beside the road, as we drove home; but in the East one is constantly thinking of the West, and we thought now of the devoted and patient Fathers who often welcomed Ch'ien Lung back to the city with pageants strung out, so one hears, from the Summer Palace to the threshold of Peking—a distance of some nine or ten miles. Clockwork figures were specially constructed for the occasion, and went through complicated manœuvres as he approached. Ch'ien Lung acquired a fondness for these spectacles, and the Jesuits were seldom without work, which he pressed them to complete in the shortest time. Mimic sea-fights were another of their inspirations, and palace courtyards were flooded for the purpose. Their astronomical science was also valued, and they built an observatory on the wall of the Tartar City.

Again my memory brings me forward to the summer months. From the ramparts which command the Legation Quarter, the Observatory can be seen but not approached, for at certain points the wall is barricaded. You walk as far as the block-house in the angle, and thence, over a corner of the town, catch sight of a squat edifice against the sky, crowded with strange-looking gigantic instruments. I made the journey there one sultry day by rickshaw. It was a hot dead-quiet afternoon and from the Observatory, to which I had climbed by a steep ramp, lanes and houses stretched shimmering and deserted. At least, there was little sign of life. Cicadæ, in trees under the parapet, still kept up their merciless stridulation which resembles the hiss of fat in some huge frying pan, magnified to the volume of a muffled roar.

No other sound; nobody about. The great useless empty wall down which I looked marched direct towards the dilapidated block-house, turned at right angles and approached a distant gate tower, reappearing stiff and precise to join the next. The brickwork of the Observatory was very hot, and the brazen surface of the massive instruments which filled the platform was hot, almost scorching, to the hand; astrolabes, a mighty globe embossed with gilt, marking the zodiac, the planets and lesser stars. There were many of which I did not know the name; but their size and the opulent pedestals on which they stood— knotted dragons supported the heaviest pieces—all cast in solid lustrous bronze, gave them a supernatural, slightly terrifying dignity. Star-gazing, for those who do not practice it and whose astronomy is confined to Ursa Major, has always a somewhat necromantic air. One learns that the Chaldeans observed the stars; imagination promptly casts across its screen the picture of a bearded man on a white house-top, tall and solitary under a host of icy planets which flash larger and bluer than we see them now. . . . Every astronomer has the prestige of the first Chaldean, and the Jesuits, who built the little Observatory, populating it with these intricate brazen skeletons, grouped around the starry globe which was their map, take on, since they have vanished, a mysterious magnitude. The walls and the gate towers may crumble away; it will need a determined vandal to wreck the instruments.

CHAPTER VI

AT A PLAY

Elsewhere the spoilers are working fast. Jehol, the great hunting-palace beyond the Wall, one of the most beautiful and the strangest of Imperial dwellings, has been reduced to a mere ruin in twenty years. The soldiers have settled down on it like locusts. An ex-brigand, now dignified as general, has demolished many pavilions for their precious wood; the immense lake has been allowed to run dry; while the only sign of prosperity in the whole province are the glimmering white fields of tall opium poppies.

In Peking, too, roofs sag and pillars crumble. A visit to the Temple of Confucius, the Hall of the Classics and other monuments of the Imperial epoch, is a dream of desolation and declining splendour; grassy courtyards, cells and cloisters filled with rubbish, deep moats, crossed by bow-shaped marble bridges, nowadays clogged with weed and thick with scum. A single vague custodian hovers around. In the Imperial Palace you could walk for several hours, in and out of the huge empty desolate courts, up terraces and through pavilions large and small, unaccompanied save by the rhythm of your own footsteps.

Architecture, in the Western sense, scarcely exists, for the individual architect never emerges. Insensibly lines are modified and lines are exaggerated; tiled roofs hump against the sky or sink with majestically spreading eaves. The very subtlety of this age-long evolution rouses a feeling of impatient emptiness in the Western mind. One demands pyrotechnics, obvious brilliance; and just as the elaborate ritual they were built to accommodate has lent an air of fixity to Buddhist shrines, so the ceremonious existence of the Chinese Emperor —as remote from life as the monarch of a playing card—has expressed itself in the frozen formalism of his official residence.

I have mentioned the extreme intricacy of the plan. Behind the large courtyard already described lies another equally extensive and deep-sunk, prefacing the white marble Peony Terrace— three terraces with embrasures between the steps, each embrasure containing a bronze urn. Amply proportioned, nobly conceived, it is poor in detail. Down the centre of every flight of steps is laid a sort of solid sculptural carpet, embossed with the usual design of furious dragons. Its balustrades, sufficiently elegant in outline, are fretfully ornamented, when one comes near enough to examine them, with a knobbed pattern reminiscent of English crochet work.

Above the terrace is a throne-room or audience chamber. Round columns, encrusted with gold leaf, soar up to an elaborately coffered ceiling and are joined there by a rather meaningless wealth of brackets. They are heavy and yet somehow out of scale; the decoration is ponderous but insignificant. This interior, like so many Eastern interiors, seems the reverse, or *wrong*, side of a great building. The sense of symmetry, spent in grouping pavilions and

o   209

gateways, seems to have been exhausted before the architect crossed the threshold.

The inside of a Chinese house is often comfortless, and
doubly sad are the apartments of the last Emperor. Here
he lived on till not many years ago, tolerated by the
Republic which had dethroned him, sole surviving coral
insect of an enormous reef. The courtyards he inhabited
are very small. We peered through a glazed but dusty
window and made out in the obscurity a brass bedstead,
some timepieces, a bronze statue of Marshal Joffre, among
bric-à-brac in enamel, jade and ormulu. They were as
pathetic as the feathers and down of an old nest; but the
courtyards, though not large, are rather gay, with columns papered and painted a sage green. Further on, the
blind narrow red-walled passages suggested the coming
and going of crafty eunuchs. . . .

The Temple of Heaven is a long ride from the Imperial
Palace, and stands in a sequestered angle of the outer city.
All around it is a quiet leafy park, and in a broad umbrage-
ous avenue beneath the trees, I remember the tripping
gait of several hoopoes, like Red Indians with their lofty
painted crests which wagged and flickered behind them as
they stalked away. Chinese actors come here to rehearse
their roles; and on the grass we caught sight of an old man
who sat teaching the Sword Dance to a young pupil, getting up now and then to explain a step and using his
walking stick instead of a naked sword.

The temple itself, with its three tiers of blue umbrellas,
is less beautiful than the terrace on which it stands and the
twin gateways that admitted us to the sacred precincts. A
paved avenue leads direct to the Altar of Heaven, three
circular terraces superimposed which look down on the

ornate Temple of Agriculture. Wonderfully spacious the concentric plan of those three terraces, their knobbed balustrades of crystalline marble and shallow flights of gradually mounting steps. They seem to embrace the sky and welcome the sun; they have an air, seldom met with in Chinese temples, of rising beyond the needs of the official cult, of escaping with their geometrical simplicity from the deadening and precise touch of conventional usage. . . .

The young dancer was still rehearsing as we walked back. We had already visited a Chinese theatre in Shanghai, a large noisy crowded sweltering place in which the lights did not go down when the curtain rose and attendants brought tea and steaming face-cloths—the latter tossed adroitly through the air to any patron who took the trouble to lift his hand. Our view of the stage, and the actors and orchestra, was continually intersected by flying towels; and the enthusiasm a single actor might evoke could only be gauged from a slight lull in the continuous hubbub.

It was the same at a theatre in Peking. The performance had been under way since the afternoon and would not finish, we were told, till nearly midnight. It was like an interminable undifferentiated frieze, like a film contrived to punish the ghost of a filmgoer, rattled off with break-neck rapidity but never ending. Actors marched and countermarched behind the footlights; generals and emperors, in portentous quivering head-dresses, black beards extending silkily past the waist, stamped through on their thick-soled massive boots, which they lifted as though walking under water, and delivered themselves of harsh minatory harangues. Their faces were boldly painted to resemble masks; their gestures expressed Brobdingnagian

PEKING

pride—whether it was the gesture of gravely stroking their long beards—beards so all-concealing that they resembled yashmaks—or a gesture of concentrated disapprobation, with raised elbow as when Zeus hurls a thunderbolt.

How different from the solemn decency of the Japanese stage, on which the actors wear kimono of rich silk and every property is as solid and sumptuous as art can make it! Good taste there is an almost paralysing obsession; these actors took their seats on rickety chairs before a curtain sewn with sequins and badly hung. The orchestra, in soiled and greasy Western hats, had congregated at one end of the lighted stage, and swilled tea, smoked and talked while playing their instruments. Gongs and cymbals were incessantly kept busy; their brassy din floated out across the audience and very often the high-pitched bawling of the actors reached us in a mere tremulous wraith of sound, a faint scratch upon its hard metallic surface.

It plucked the nerves and set them tingling under the scalp. Still, as brief sections of an endless frieze, strange personages marched across our view—emperors going to battle or making love, concubines, prime ministers, scheming emissaries, gods and barbarians and innocent girls, dressed in the archaic fashions of the T'ang court, beflagged, brightly bedizened and thick-booted, spangle-trimmed, huge in bulk or slender and willowy, surrounded by a multitude of gauzy scarves. They spoke against the music, seldom with it; warriors like the Ogre of a pantomime, rolling out a prodigious volume of wrath, women and maidens in an unutterably shrill falsetto, faint but piercing, which ran a needle through the ear-drums.

Thus the Fairy: her voice was sweet for all its shrillness,

and she was clad in a soft robe with drifting sleeves. Two pheasant's feathers, some five or six feet long, arched back from the middle of her coiffure and undulated gracefully to her buoyant walk. The Fairy might have provided a solution; she fenced with and defeated a black-faced giant, and afterwards, whirling her veils and her slender sword, stepped out into an intricate surprising dance, at which the audience grew comparatively quiet—so miraculous was the glistening pattern that she wove.

But this was all; the hubbub started again, and the Fairy—a famous actor, it appeared—went swaying off with gossamer indirectness, while more generals pranced forward to the sound of gongs. . . . I distracted myself by looking about the house. The orchestra were wiping their faces and drinking tea, and privileged persons poked in from behind the stage. Towel-purveyors continued to stroll among the audience, collecting and dispensing their damp cloths. Family parties were established in small boxes; old women with triangular bound feet, shaped like the feet of a Dutch doll, who puffed cigarettes and stared beadily, sometimes shifting a comb to scratch their heads, and young men in white gowns and panama hats, accompanied by girls in flowered silk.

The younger women were dressed to an identical fashion, a narrow tubular sheath from ankle to chin, light-coloured and moulded supply to their bodies, giving them a flat-chested long-limbed elegance which they exaggerated by cutting their hair short and slipping large bracelets over their hands. They were made up with a discreet but determined emphasis, and their sharp eyes, pencilled eyebrows and worldly carriage would have not been inappropriate in a French theatre, for they had none of the squabby shapelessness of a Japanese, none of her startled diffidence and nervous mannerisms, possessing, even to the point of angularity, all the features that have determined Western modes.

They had a 'smartness' to which no Japanese could aspire, since Japanese women are almost invariably long-waisted, plump but flat-bosomed at the same time. Very touching are the breasts of a Japanese mother. From childhood swaddled round by the tight *obi*, their breasts do not develop until lactation; and a working woman who gives suck in a crowded tram—often to a child with a school cap, a sturdy and belligerent little boy—reveals a perfect globe like the breast of a Madonna, on which the gluttonous nurseling eagerly hangs.

Japanese women have an artificial naivety, a *niaiserie*, attractive or the reverse, inculcated by many years of self-effacement. Shyness and suppression is in their blood; and the kept dancing girl, with a European lover, is sometimes as coy and abashed as the virtuous wife. Chinese women are genuinely sophisticated; take our friends' friend, for example, Madame C, a Manchu princess of the old regime, educated in Paris at the turn of the century, who looks back to the court of the Empress Dowager and still laughs at stories about the eunuchs. They had no political influence, she says; they were stupid and often jeered at for their deficiency; *à propos* she remembers a little pun, made by the young Empress who enjoyed teasing them. . . .

She recalls sledging parties across the lake; Old Buddha —she was really not unkind; one cannot believe the stories of her cruelty—in sable-trimmed robes upon the sled, pulled by eunuchs and some adventurous maids-in-waiting, among whom, as it happens, was herself. During the summer, eunuch boatmen poled their barge; and a photograph, which she has presented to our friends, shows the Empress sitting amidships in a high chair—you can see the formidable length of her uncut fingernails and the deep lines on her haggard ancient face—surrounded by her ladies in their summer frocks and her eunuchs in shady hats and voluminous gowns.

An acute profile, dark eyes and a pallid skin; her black hair is shorn closely in an 'Eton crop'; she speaks French more readily than she speaks English: 'I do not like to go out often nowadays. *Mes compatriotes* look at me so oddly. I remember when the Palace was quite different; I should not care to see it as it is now. . . .' Till recently she was a heavy smoker, but it made her ill: 'pendant deux années j'ai mangé presque rien. . . .' Her husband, a Southern Chinese gentleman with charming urbane manners and a slow smile, has the puzzled and perceptibly subdued look that comes of long marriage to a brilliant wife.

Or take a daughter of the Peking *bourgeoisie*. Miss T is a beauty in her own world and had accompanied us that evening to the theatre. She is very attractive; she would be attractive in any gathering, partly because the consciousness of charm lends a certain smooth benignity to those who enjoy it—they are sorry for and perhaps touched by the unfavoured—and partly because her features in themselves have a distinction that is achieved by very few. They are agreeably—yet very slightly—mongoloid; eyes slanting enough to be characteristic, high cheekbones and a delicate small nose, teeth white as peeled almonds and as regularly shaped, lips very red and rather full which she draws back when she laughs or expresses pleasure.

Best of all are her wrists and pointed hands. I have never seen a thinner or neater wrist, attached so symmetrically to the arm. Her movements are accomplished and decided; and her attitude, while watching the stage spectacle, pointing with her fan or explaining a song, was nicely blended of interest and mild ennui; for she would much rather have been dancing at the hotel to the sugared music of a not very good American band.

She is reputed to be the mistress of various Italians. It may be true; but in Peking, as in other cities, virginity is only credited on definite proof. . . . At last we got up to leave the theatre; and Miss T, saying good-night and entering a rickshaw, reminded me of Tchehov's story called *The Beauties*, an account of two girls he had once seen, against a background of village posting-house and station platform, who spread around them that curious saddened stillness which is now and then our response to physical charm. . . .

Our rickshaws swerved away in opposite directions; the coolie's feet went thudding over the dust. Peking, late at night, is very silent. Very soon we should be catching the train home, and I thought almost with hatred of the return journey. Why is Japan, after China, so small and breathless? It is compact and clean and moderately well-governed; such cruelties as are practised are of the Western type, and, though socialists are left to languish in Tokyo jails, they are not subjected to the 'carrying-pole torture', they are not 'sliced' nor castrated nor beaten to shreds; merely thumped and occasionally garotted by a zealous policeman.[1]

[1] For an interesting account of Japanese police methods, during the confusion which followed the great Earthquake, see Young: *Japan under Taisho Tenno*. Allen & Unwin. 1928. p. 300 and elsewhere.

Cruelty pervades the air of a Chinese town. The Chinese are grossly ignorant and self-satisfied, dependant on but contemptuous of the 'foreign devil', venal and narrow minded, inveterate bigots. They have a long literature which instils official rectitude, and a long record of dishonest and greedy functionaries. . . . So, at least, I have been told by English friends. Yet, mysteriously but unmistakably, 'one can breathe', and China remains oddly sympathetic; peasant children who run naked in the hot weather, old men and stalwart coolies stripped to the waist who sit outside mud cottages and smoke and talk, while cicadas hum and sizzle in the feathery trees and brown-coated desert camels go lurching past. Life here is reduced to its lowest terms; every man attends to his own business, his family, his own comfort, his own pleasure, and takes his pet bird for an airing in the cool of the day. Amid the endless meddling of modern world, perfect cynicism has much to recommend it.

PART IV
KYOTO

CHAPTER I

THE ANCIENT CAPITAL

Our return to Kobe was accomplished in a gale; large cabin trunks slid and tilted about the floor, while overcoats and dresses hanging from pegs leaned out and swayed back with a sickly rhythm. Now and then, we heard the crash of falling crockery; bells rang incessantly along the passage; and yesterday's cups and plates under the bed rattled dismally to and fro as the steamer lurched.

After Shimonosekei, there was a period of blessed stillness, for, appropriately enough, the entrance to Japan is through the narrow and fiordlike Inland Sea, scattered thick with a thousand islands of distinctive beauty that proclaim themselves at first sight as Japanese. They suggest the islands of an exquisite wash drawing, steep volcanic eminences fledged with pines, dark crests two-dimensional and clear-cut—at a distance they seem to float above the haze that hangs as smooth as milk across the water. They are more beautiful than any Grecian archipelago, of every shape, every size and degree of fantasy. And nature slowly unwinds her improvization, like an artist with two hands unwinding a scroll. . . .

Next Kobe, all bustle and specious modernism; we boarded an electric train for Kyoto where the cherry trees were in flower and tourists hummed. How familiar and how *safe*, to our enlightened eyes! In the lounge of the large comfortless *hôtel de luxe*, white-coated and self-important Japanese circled eagerly about the swarm of foreign arrivals, bringing them tea and confusing orders and accepting tips. So efficient, at any rate in their own view, so helpful yet so anxious to strike a bargain; news-papers and films and picture postcards, lacquers and ivories and other trophies of the Ancient East.

It was raining when we set foot in the hotel, and the rain turned to sleet as we looked out. Behind a veil of grey sleety driving mist, the summits of flowering cherry trees that dotted the town resembled pink dabs of *poudre de riz* which might melt and run away if the storm continued. But it cleared up, and the evening was calm and fine. All around us the wooded hills emerged, a dark rim humped roughly against the horizon; and the many rivu-lets that wander through Kyoto added a trickle of music to the quiet air.

Clean and sweet-scented after the storm, Kyoto seemed a pleasant place that evening. We walked under a huge *torii*, salmon-red, and found ourselves in the big forecourt of a Shinto temple, strewn with freshly raked glimmering white sand. A cherry tree had blossomed beneath the ter-race; some trees bear blossoms on leafless boughs and lose their petals when the leaves begin to show; while others— our tree was of this variety—produce blossoms and foliage at same instant, small shining bronze-pink leaves among the flowers setting off their faint nacreous rosy gleam. There were many trees in temple courtyards and beside

DETAIL OF A WALL-PAINTING AT HŌRYŪJI

the streets, many temples, standing apart or among the houses. Here was a vermilion-painted Inari shrine, a few steps from the crowded bustling pavement—jaunty stone foxes on granite pedestals, a man audibly at prayer in front of an image and the paper windows of the priest's house brilliantly lit—and here, on a platform above the town, approached by a winding cobbled avenue, was silence only troubled by the devout errand boy who briefly clapped his hands and tugged at a bell.

The lamps of Kyoto started to spangle in the dusk. . . . Perhaps we had found the 'real Japan'. Was it more real than the hideous hotel dining room, with its waitresses in bright kimono and smart sashes, its swarm of English spinsters and American matrons, effusively comparing notes and consulting guides? Kyoto is the 'art-centre' of Japan; and the reception clerk, who cashed our travellers' cheques, was always telephoning from his office in the entrance-hall for permits to visit a palace or a garden.

'Very historic, very picturesque,' he said. We had decided to begin our sightseeing with the Nijo Castle, formerly the residence of the Shogun in Kyoto, the building in which he expressed his pride and wealth, when he alone was the real master of Japan and the Emperor its mere religious and titular sovereign. White ramparts and white corner towers across a moat; the massive mediæval doors studded with bronze admitted us to a spacious pebbled yard. Under the steep commanding roofs of the main edifice, we walked straight into a series of big apartments, used as living-rooms by the Shogun's powerful feudatories when they came with their retinues to pay him court.

All open on a wide verandah passage; and this passage, which separates them from the garden, has underfoot what is prettily known as a 'nightingale floor', polished boards that squeaked musically as we moved along, looking into one apartment after another. Each has a different scheme of decoration. The Shogun employed artists of the Kano school, who frescoed the thin partitions dividing the rooms with the bright colours and wreathing shapes that suited their style. Too lavish, too exuberant, was their virtuosity; stripy tigers, against a dim golden ground, roll and leap with kittenish *joie de vivre*; peacocks perch on the limbs of an ancient tree; sparrows bicker and dash through sprays of blossom. The brushwork is somewhat feeble, though very accomplished, while the ventilation lattices under the roof—the ceiling itself is coffered, gilded and painted—are carved with similar motifs by Hidari Jingoro, a semi-mythical Grinling Gibbons of Japan.

The result is perilously theatrical; and the Shogun's audience-chambers, which lie beyond, are almost vulgar, so histrionic is their setting, a broad dais and behind it a deep alcove—black lacquer, gold and painted screens. Ostentation may be amusing if contrived with skill; but to this palace, as to the mausolea at Nikko, clings a certain deadening atmosphere of determined opulence. The Shoguns, who had won their power at the edge of the sword, had still many of the traits of artistic *parvenus*.

After the pomp and theatrical circumstance of the Nijo Castle, the Emperor's palace seems poverty-stricken and small. With an effect of rather irritating good taste, it stands back behind its modest outer courtyards, a plain entry, as simple as that of an inn, giving access to a bare unfurnished corridor. Other apartments are on an equally subdued scale; there is the courtiers' dining-room, a cheerless oblong chamber only enlivened by the red braid which binds the *tatami*, and next door the private rooms of the Emperor and Empress, slightly secluded in a pavilion of their own.

Little plan; pavilions are strung round courtyards and linked together by exposed and windy passages—often an open bridge crossing a gap—with underfoot dark musically squeaking boards. A bare elegance; but what penetrating discomfort! It was a spring day; the sun was pale and the air was fresh; and I thought of days when heavy snow had fallen, and the court ladies, indigent and aristocratic, must have shuffled in the cumbrous winter silks backwards and forwards on some errand for their mistress, through the draughts, across a stinging wedge of air that smelt of snow drifted deep in the empty yard. . . . Still worse, on days of black and dripping thaw. Winter at Kyoto is always harsh; and many torments, devised for the Buddhist hell, would have been less intolerable than the splendid routine of these poor ladies, numbed and chapped whether they moved or remained sitting in a palace which is as frigid as any charnel.

Very odd that in the name of pride and sanctity human beings should have invented such an inferno! But human greatness and human idiocy are closely connected; and, myself preserved from occupying any niche in it, I could not be altogether sorry to think they had. On the one hand, the arrogant selflessness of devoted courtiers, on the other the conscious majesty of the Imperial insect, kept this hive in motion for many hundred years; while the Emperor, usually neglected and often poor, continued to perform his functions with sublime automatism. . . .

The hurried glimpse which we were allowed of his private apartments threw some light on that bleak and limited destiny. The window-flaps of a large pavilion had been raised, and looking through we saw a bare and lofty chamber, appointed with chilly sacerdotal gorgeousness. There was a striped tent, its silk curtains looped aside and held in place by a pair of lion-dogs; and under this, so we learned, the Imperial pontifex had enacted various ceremonies for the good of his realm. On a polished cement slab, sprinkled with sand, another ritual had been performed every morning; here the ministrant had his feet upon the earth, without the troublesome necessity of leaving the room.

Smaller cells actually housed the Imperial couple, low rooms with brightly painted sliding doors, opened and shut with tassels of rich silk. Their decoration was pretty but insignificant, and in weaker taste than the decoration of the Nijo Castle, Chinese sages at home in a romantic landscape, flying clouds on a heaven of cobalt blue. . . . For the real charm of the buildings one must look outside, and walk round to admire the enclosure at different angles. It was as unpretentious as an English stable yard, with its white pavilions half-timbered in black or red, its roofs made of strips of greyish bark, laid so as to form a heavy thatch, supported on delicate square columns, green rush-blinds rolled up in every door. A tiny stream tinkled through a channel and, flanking the steps of the coronation hall, were a meagre flowering cherry tree and a large orange shrub. No setting could be more perfectly in contrast with the ripe oppressive luxury that surrounded the Shogun. . . .

Ostentation reached its height under Yoshimitsu; but it was this Shogun—how characteristic of the breed, the

scion of a new family turning to art, though mere display
has satisfied his predecessors!—who resigned and with-
drew to his Golden Pavilion, there to cultivate the aris-
tocracy of the spirit. The *Kinkaku* is a landmark in Japanese æstheticism, a three-storeyed, plainly built wooden
structure, almost unornamented, on the edge of a small
lake.

Examined through Western eyes, it means little or
nothing. Admirably suited to its position, without a
doubt, nicely balanced, unobtrusive, quiet and elegant.
To a Japanese just that *quietness* is its appeal; for *yugen*—the
quality beneath the surface—may be arrived at in architecture as in No by a scrupulous avoidance of apparent
effort. The architect is subtle by seeming plain; and, as
prophets of the East from Jesus to Gandhi have spoken of
the strength that lies in weakness and of the mountains
that can be dislodged by inner rectitude, so a Japanese
attacks the problems of æsthetic conduct by emphasizing
the virtues of the unexpressed.

Thus the beauty of the *Kinkaku* is implicit. Two styles
of architecture are combined; the top and the bottom
storey are in different manners, while the storey that di-
vides them is cleverly mixed. From a Western point of
view the distinction is slight; and the *Kinkaku*, with other
products of the same period—the period that saw the
blossoming of No—has a charm somewhat diluted by
insipidity. Its manners are uncomfortably perfect, its dis-
cretion so consummate that it offends. 'After you!' it
seems to protest to surrounding nature, and shrinks away
into its background of lawn and trees.

Should a building take precedence of nature? The
Golden Pavilion insists emphatically that it should not.

It should be a detail, and a quiet detail, of the landscape. Bleached and silvery, the ancient summer-house beside the pond, where every rock and every reflection has its place—*knows* its place, one might say, and has learned its lesson—makes room with exquisite courtesy for natural objects. But then nature has been schooled to return the compliment; it smiles back at the frail building in its midst, the smooth pond sedulously catching its graceful image and handing it up again as if it enjoyed the role of courtier, the gnarled trees stepping apart a respectful distance as if anxious to avoid a suspicion of familiarity.

By comparison a formal garden would be unsophisticated. Here not an island and not a tree, but has a value and a purpose of its own. The rocks have been carefully chosen for their shapes, and each slab bears its name in neat characters—symbolic or fantastic—on a little board. Yet the intention—and the effect—is deliberately wild; it is the microcosm of a still virgin Japanese scene. The measure of its sublime sophistication is its fidelity to the observed groupings of forest and shore.

The Japanese landscape is susceptible to such management, and, if native artists in studying its moods have usually become the victims of a mawkish formula, one may add that only a race of artistic giants could have conquered the temptation it put in their way. Few landscapes are more exquisitely stylized; even the sea as it beats against the coast, where Japan lies open to the Pacific surge, has broken off innumerable fragments of living rock, gnawed, splintered and channelled from below, while above it has left them barely sufficient foothold to afford purchase to the dragonish roots of a gaunt pine.

There are pines on the islets out at sea; and inland,

along the abrupt volcanic hills that huddle down across the plain towards the shore, like some drove of migrant animals traversing the country, they stand up and bristle black against the sunset. They rise solitary and contemplative on lonely heights, or lean dizzily from the lip of a sheer precipice. . . .

The pine haunts the mountains and the shore; but the bamboo, on the verge of the farmer's land, in a warm valley, behind his conical thatched roof, clicks and rustles dryly under the breeze, nodding its tall panache of feathery foliage. The driven snow clings precariously among its crests, till it bends over and the drift falls with a soft thud.

Yes, nature is characteristic, and so are the seasons. Snow comes down in the winter sudden and deep; it obliterates the aspiring temple roofs and, when a thaw begins, slides gradually from the eaves—a tablecloth half dragged on to the floor—thick icicles dripping and glistening at its ragged edge. Clouds of blossom diversify the rainy spring. The wet season itself, the hateful Nyubai, is not without its own especial charm; the rain arrows straight from an indigo heaven in long vertical lances that pit the earth.

The summer is steamy and oppressive; but during the autumn the eternal dampness leaves the air and the country is beautiful as at no other time. It is particularly beautiful in the neighbourhood of Mount Fuji. The days are crystal clear and the nights are cold; there is a scent of burning wood upon the wind, and the rumble of a waterwheel round every farm. The steep thatch of the peasants' houses looks smooth and glossy, and, under the roofs, yellow cobs of indian corn have been hung up to dry in a deep fringe. The orange ruddy globes of ripe persimmons burn isolated in a grey framework of leafless boughs.

Heavy snow has fallen on Fujiyama. It gathers in its skirts from the surrounding plain and rises, plumed with white, across the sky—faultless, utterly symmetrical. 'Like a fan,' said the student who showed me his poem; like some majestic and inimitable commonplace, conceived for the delight of mediocrity, since it is banal and supremely beautiful all at once. How unfortunate have been the Japanese in their great mountain! Etna, with three sweeping lines that trail up from the Mediterranean shore, to end in a truncated cone of ice and a faint wisp of vapour filming and spreading, achieves an effect of almost supernatural magnitude. It dominates and electrifies the entire landscape; the actual curves that compose it are squat and broken, but, in drawing one's eye slowly towards the ice-cap, give an impression of incalculable height and distance. Fuji is a fan or an inverted flower. It drifts high overhead beyond the clouds, and sometimes, should one approach when the sun is sinking and the plain beneath is full of shadow and pricked with light, it emerges, a clear crest and sloping shoulder, frigid and pale as if it formed a separate universe.

But it is dead; one can never forget that; while the pure curve which it thrusts up towards the sky is too finished, too glassy smooth, to be quite credible. We had spent a week-end motoring round its base, cold sunny days in early October, fresh-coloured and sharp-scented among the foothills, where the woods, at a first touch of frost, had begun to redden—either a fiery scarlet red or red that had the quality of a vivid rust-stain; beeches a transparent golden yellow, fluttering leaves as light and luminous as discs of foil.

There are many lakes in the district about Fuji; but they are less beautiful—though very beautiful they are, with their rocky islets and the tall sighing nodding grass which grows down to the water's edge if the shore is flat—than a lake in the mountains above Nikko whither we had gone to escape the summer heat. Lake Chuzenji is some six or seven miles long, and at one end the conical bulk of a sacred mountain, visited by companies of white-clad pilgrims, throws its reflection boldly across the water, which is chilly and greenish-dark and very deep. A monstrous salamander is said to live at the bottom, and not long ago a Japanese naval diver, sent down to look for a drowned man, reappeared panic-stricken on the surface, declaring that it had swum past him as he descended.

Besides its salamander, it has also a foreign colony, at whose expense a whole book might be written—telling how secretaries and chargés d'affaires steer their shallops furiously before the wind in a succession of races which last all summer; white sails and pink sails traversing the lake, ruffling the splendid image of its wooded shores and converging upon the tiny island named Formosa round which they turn, or attempt to turn and come to grief. Rudders foul, booms jibe, shouts are exchanged. The events of the day are threshed out in the club-house; such a pity Colonel So-and-So lost his temper; M. de S. has no idea of sailing a boat and seems to think of nothing but his complexion, which he anoints perseveringly with olive oil. *Pas sportif* . . . almost as bad as a dyspeptic *confrère* who does not leave his hotel bedroom till mid-day and then saunters down, melancholy and preoccupied, in a straw boater, carrying a silver-mounted walking stick, as if he had stepped straight from some old photograph of the Ostend *plage*.

Ambassadors are fatherly but remote. For the most part, like English 'nannies' at the seaside, they are content to sit on the beach and watch the fun, occasionally starting races and presenting challenge cups. One of them surprisingly had brought a friend, and the efforts of various anglo-saxon dignitaries to avoid taking cognisance of Mrs. Z, large, blowsy and blonde in flowered chiffon, were a pretty instance of ambassadorial tact. They were as blind to the velleities of their subordinates—Japanese girls in European frocks, hidden away in the upper storeys of wooden houses and spirited out, when dusk fell, for a breath of air. . . .

But I have divagated—I was writing of Fujiyama, of its too finished and all too obvious grace, and of the landscape garden which surrounds the Golden Pavilion and epitomizes the characteristic of the Japanese scene. Personal preferences are least obnoxious when undisguised; and I must confess that, although Japan as far as I saw it has passages of incomparable beauty, they gave my imagination little scope, that never once did it expand with a sense of freedom as in the roomy dishevelled vastness of Northern China.

CHAPTER II

STATUES

J apan is the product of art but not its material. From
every feature—you might say from every line—human ingenuity has drained the essence, till what one
sees is not a stretch of pebbly road, among rice fields
in which the peasants are at work, so much as a complete
colour print by Hiroshige, one of his many facile pictures
of the Road to Yedo, only lacking the itinerant feudal lord
with his armed retainers and half-naked coolie chairmen.

Great art has a way of transcending its object, of leaving a margin, an unexploited residue. The domestic and
popular arts of the Japanese race, encouraged by the
strange surroundings in which they developed, have
fastened on the beauty of the outer world, pinning it down
and spreading out its wings, just as they have stylized the
charm and oddity of their own existence. The Japanese
landscape has become a brilliant painted panel to guard
Japan from froward foreign contacts. . . .

Hills as flat as the hills upon a screen. All landscapes
acquire the character of their inhabitants, and the Japanese is no exception to this rule, indeed a striking proof of
its validity. But then climate has added something to the

effect, misty and vague—even the light of the sunniest days is less distinct than one supposes when taking photographs, and hides and softens more than it reveals. Except in autumn, the air is always damp, the result being a blurred and misted view that induces an equally nebulous state of mind. A stranger, puzzled and irritated at first, slowly sinks into the mood of acquiescence.

It was in that mood we walked about Kyoto. Almost a year—we had known Japan almost a year, its rainy season, its summer, its enchanting autumn and the fierce blizzards that descended during January and made our white cats look yellowish against the snow, piled up beneath the warped and draughty screens. It was like living in a summer house amid snowdrifts. But the icicles had begun to weep, the snow had melted. We had escaped and now, on our return, Japan was, if not lovable, at least familiar.

Familiarity is in the end an endearing trait. Japanese ladies, fur tippets about their necks which were washed a purplish shade with *o shiroi*, shuffled past, carrying reticules and cheap umbrellas. Dawdling students, with books under their arms, done up in enormous bandana kerchiefs, and black respirators masking their noses and mouths, seemed to hover, as Japanese students always do, between the different worlds that claimed their enlightened suffrage. A man with a performing ape, a street musician. . . . We knew it all, and how the taxi-driver would behave, how he would pretend he understood, then turn round and gape for further directions, producing a faint grin of utmost incredulity.

From the Golden Pavilion we drove across Kyoto to a temple, in a large park on the opposite side, bustling with a cheerful aimless holiday crowd. Pale blossoms sprinkled the soft air and on the flagged paths, which traverse the temple enclosure, clatter and clap went incessant wooden clogs. Country people out to see the sights; the man ambled a pace or two in advance, his best kimono girded up around his knees, a European straw hat on the back of his head, while his women, as small and drab as a group of pea-hens, picked their way at a short distance, laughing and gossiping. Or they all sat down in one of the many restaurants. . . .

We left the austere temples on the hill and, through many winding neatly gardened paths, reached a sort of fair-ground inside the gate, loud with music and perfumed with the scent of rice wine. The fair centred about the trunk of an ancient cherry tree, a giant, but so debilitated by age and renown that it leant on a multitude of stout crutches. Photographers were active with tripod cameras, and grinning peasants and sedate *bourgeois* and bevies of schoolboys—the last pompously conducted by plump professors—took turns in posing groups to be sent home. Few pedestrians unaccompanied this evening; they admired the tree, as they did all else, by squads and companies.

But the venerable ruin stood alone. Three limbs rose clear of its twisted trunk; and these three, ancient and gnarled and strongly supported, were clothed in a fine veil of dripping flowers—fine as osprey, fine as the foliage of a willow—which fell sheer and delicate towards the earth and seemed to illumine the faces of the passers-by. Next the gate was a row of canvas booths; under gaudily striped red and white awnings, on a trestle floor covered with rush mats, people were carousing to the accompaniment of loud-speakers that trolled forth the latest geisha songs.

Noise, amiability, good behaviour; casks of wine were heaped up at the back of the tents, and a sweetish fume of alcohol pervaded the air which was so humid that it gave scents a haunting pungency. Festivals are still holidays in Japan. While some holiday-makers drank and laughed, others, as they passed under the red gate, halted to perform their devotions at a shrine.

Placid and to the point their devotion was. In the dusk of the huge open temple front, above the altar prettily set with coloured offerings—rice loaves, white and pink, fruit and blossoms—Shinto mirrors glimmered through the twilight. The devout bowed deeply and clapped their hands; each took a copper or silver coin and tossed it in over the well-worn lustrous mats. The sound of coins falling on to the floor made a pleasant rainy patter as we drew near.

It was a warm hazy tranquillizing moment. Next day we set out for Nara and Horyuji, thus moving back some centuries in time. Nara was the capital before Kyoto; then Kyoto was superseded by Kamakura—Kyoto remaining a nominal and religious pivot—and Kamakura by Yedo, the modern Tokyo, where the Emperor came to reside after the Restoration. Feudal Japan was founded and destroyed; but, in the period antecedent to the feudal epoch, an art little known by Europeans had time to take roots in Japanese life. It was an art still innocent of *japonaiserie*, less characteristic but infinitely more vital.

Its traces are not to be discovered all at once. Nara, when we had visited it with the Professor, had a sentimental and mildly romantic charm, its tame deer wandering under the trees, its long ascent between an avenue of stone lanterns, to the new bright vermilion Shinto shrine. The Professor bought some knick-knacks to hang on his watch-chain, but though he escorted us to the temple of the Great Buddha he did not suggest that we should visit the museum. Had he done so, his knowledge of the English essayists and championship of the Young Men's Christian Association scarcely qualified him as an exponent of Japanese art.

He stood touchingly for something he called 'progress', and like the majority of progressive Japanese—progressive in the educational, material sense—was further from Western thought and Western values than an actor or archæologist who spoke no English. By minimizing differences he merely exaggerated them; but if on that first occasion we had left his side—and the chilly strangeness that enveloped our attempts at intimacy—it is possible that behind the doors of the Nara museum our bewilderment might have lost its immediate edge.

Suppose one stepped in unprepared. It is not a large place and many of the exhibits are on loan from temples and monasteries in the surrounding countryside, where they inhabit some dark and ancient shrine. They have emerged for a brief space into full daylight; temple guardians flourishing swords and trampling demons. . . . But these, though often vigorous, one can pass by, moving on towards a tall wooden statue which has long hair and a broad naked back and seems curiously reminiscent of a statue one knows. Is it of a Greek charioteer, so simple and straight and almost stiff?

The next is considerably more florid; its robes and the long stole crossing its shoulders wave out in a delicate exuberant line, while its fingers, which just meet in the movement of prayer, are soft and curving as its smooth impassive face under the high-piled, flowered and plaited top-knot. This statue, too, awakes some memory, and the third suddenly fires a train of thought. Henceforward one sees the Buddhist saints and demigods lit up by a dim aura of recognition.

The third is a bald-headed male figure. Its small skull and fine chinless slothlike profile run down into a thick and fleshy neck, a smooth shoulder and a suavely drooping arm which depends with pointed forefinger against the flank. Incredibly it is the Eastern cousin of a Roman Isis and, when one looks back, the other two and their companions stand out as collateral descendants of the same stock, ripened travesties of Græco-Roman sculpture, odd pilgrims from the Hellenistic world. . . .

Pilgrims who have gone far and are much changed. They have journeyed, whether through the passes or on shipboard, from Europe to Buddhist India and thence to China; from China with monks and artists to Japan. Their features you would certainly not recognize; the cheeks have pressed up beneath the eyelids and the eyes are half shut at the extreme corners, so that the whole face has acquired a look of sleepy wisdom. Their arms are no longer lean and athletic, but full-fleshed, androgynous and very supple. Their ears, pierced and stretched till they touch their shoulders, are symbolic indications of their new servitude.

But unmistakably one recognizes their parentage; they have little to show for it—the line of a pendant arm, something energetic in the attitude of the 'charioteer'—and none the less contrive to betray their origin, like bastards of royal blood in a crowd of commoners. Perhaps the

HEAD OF A STATUE OF KWANNON IN THE
NUNNERY AT HŌRYŪJI

bastards are more beautiful than the legitimate offspring; and since they are bastards it is fitting they should have made their homes on obscure altars in the vicinity of an extinct capital. They have outlived the Western tradition from which they came, but still command the reverence of Japanese rustics.

What is it that distinguishes them as works of art?—a problem which might be handed over to the experts, were the brilliance of the expert intelligence less bewildering. From the point of view of the uninstructed onlooker, the quality that determines their strange charm seems to consist in a certain infectious boldness, transcending taste as good manners transcend decorum. They have not yet felt the influence of Japanese life; and, indeed, the Japanese universe when they arrived was more fluid in form and temperament than it is now. They must have stepped across the threshold of the Empire like travelled strangers entering a small room.

They arrived in the eighth and ninth centuries. Prince Shotoku, who ruled as Regent in the seventh, had already done for his semi-barbarous contemporaries what the statesmen of the Restoration period did for Japan more than a thousand years later. He had opened it to the life of the outer world, to an influx of Buddhist priests and Chinese sages, commenting in his own hand the Lotus sutra and building the temple and monastery of Horyuji.

It was to Horyuji we meant to go after Nara, for Horyuji is a spring head of Japanese art. Thence, and from other similar foundations, it flowed out into that incomparably lovely pool to which historians have given the name of the Heian period—the period of Prince Genji's *amourettes*, the time when a message from courtier to courtier was accompanied by a shoot of green bamboo, carefully plucked, with the frost crystals still adhering, and when gentlemen chose mistresses for their calligraphy —the paradise, the apotheosis of the æsthete; which fell or crumbled gently from above, and gave way to an epoch of civil wars. . . .

Then the chivalric virtues were more prized than a taste in incense. Truculent knights and their inevitably devoted henchmen charged down into the repertoire of Kabuki plays, in clattering armour plate, on their tiny horses. . . . The new æsthetes were *parvenus* of culture— Yoshimitsu who built the Golden Pavilion and Yoshimasa, the most cultured of them all, who practised the Tea Ceremony at its silver counterpart, thus inflicting a deal of nonsense upon mankind.

Remote figures, those austerely chivalrous knights— more remote than the unknown sculptors of the eighth century, Prince Shotoku, Genji and his loves. We were making our way out of the museum, when we passed a mediæval helmet in a case, black and dully gold with a jointed neck-guard, and in front two spreading golden antennæ, delicate and slightly flattened at the tip, so that they resembled the monstrous horns of some insect warrior.

CHAPTER III

VALEDICTORY

Horyuji is lost among the rice fields; behind it stands a lonely jagged ridge, and one notices from far away along the road the thin spike of its pagoda above the trees. The monastery has never been burnt down; in the civil wars that swept across Japan, bellicose knights, with their gilded stag-beetle antennæ and heavy incrustation of lacquered harness, were responsible for the destruction of many shrines. One catches a glimpse of their disputes on a painted scroll; flames wreath out from the temple buildings and amid the confusion, where the fire is fiercest and the smoke is thickest, desperate swordsmen are engaged in parry and thrust, while mere foot-soldiers take to their heels and are cut to shreds.

But Horyuji somehow escaped the civil wars and, with the exception of a few minor changes, has altered very little since it was built. A big quadrangle surrounds the various edifices, the pagoda, the Kondo or Golden Hall, and the large majestic temple opposite the gate. It was the Kondo particularly we had come to see, a two-storeyed building standing alone, its twin roofs having a pitch of unequal altitude, its walls half-timbered in red and white. Inside, for the first moment, all is dusky; a huge altar occupies most of the floor space, peopled by a strange gathering of Buddhist statues, side by side like chance acquaintances on a railway platform. One figure is taller than the rest, taller than life and more attenuated, holding out a benignant spidery hand. Seen frontwise it is as straight and rigid as a post; but, if one steps back to get a three-quarter view, it appears to be leaning forward with gracious pliancy. From its elbows, curving down on to the pedestal, droop flat and conventionalized wreaths of drapery, while other bands, fastened at the shoulder, cross in an incised pattern above the knee. Its feet are long and narrow; its face is grave; and a broad leaf-shaped aureole behind the head is held up by a slender jointed support. It is crowned with a diadem of filagree, and has a neck-piece and bracelets of the same design.

Odd and yet captivating is the effect. Not only does the archaic charm of the statue half conceal a very accomplished rhythmic plan, as though the tall figure were alive in its tight wrappings, but the mild devotional air that seems to emanate from it is enhanced by the stiff courtesy of its solemn attitude. Kwannon may be either male or female, and this figure, so absolutely devoid of sex, controverts all anthropomorphic questioning. It is Compassion, Pity, a Saviour, what you will, a cult-object or a mere symbol as the worshipper chooses. . . .

Incidentally, its function was that of a prophet, for, although its history and origin are somewhat vague, there is no doubt that it must have reached Horyuji as an advance guard of Buddhist penetration and that it probably made the journey through Korea. It is said to belong to

THE BODHISATTVA KWANNON
TEMPLE OF HŌRYŪJI
FROM A REPLICA IN THE
BRITISH MUSEUM

the seventh century. A second Kwannon, also at Horyuji, in the nunnery where Prince Shotoku's mother lived, is thought to have been created after his death and to contain an ideal reflection of the Prince's features. But this legend, recommended by its prettiness, is scarcely credible when one examines the actual work.

No statue could be more consummately impersonal. It sits, one leg crossed over its knee, the right hand with opened fingers brushing its cheek and its head slightly bowed towards the shoulder, in an attitude of profound meditation. It might seem to be listening to its own thoughts, did the word 'thought' and all it suggests of flurried endeavour not evoke an image out of keeping with such quietude. Silence herself is not more still; its grave smoothly arched circular brows, lowered eyelids and softly indicated mouth—a faint smile appears to have settled there in perpetuity—are represented with the minimum of effort, as if the statue had taken shape during a trance. So blank, so serenely mindless, is its beauty. Age and pious handling have rubbed and polished it; incense smoke has darkened the ancient wood; and its whole surface has a subdued but glowing patina, like the irradiation of some quality from within.

To return to the background of the first statue; the inner walls of the Kondo from floor to roof are frescoed with scenes from the Buddhist paradise, still impressive in spite of age, damp and neglect. As compositions, they are grandiose and self-assured; Buddhas under spreading tasselled canopies, flanked by gracefully poised attendant figures, smaller presences hovering and looking down, among a congregation of assembled Buddhist saints, spring out from the stained and leprous

Q*

243

plaster. Shaven-headed monks raise their hands; jewelled and haloed presences whose long hair curls in serpentine tresses over their necks, whose diadems are set with lotus buds and precious stones, balance in positions of rapt ecstasy.

. The features, where they remain, are worth examining; eyebrows of incredible length and thinness, noses distinctly aquiline about the bridge, cheeks and chins almost Hellenic as to proportion, form a type never realized by the Japanese race. Indeed, so exotic is the result that some historians have suggested that the Kondo may have been decorated by a group of Indian painters. Indian, Chinese or Japanese? The truth, it has been recently pointed out, probably lies somewhere between the three, for at the time when these wall-paintings were executed Buddhist art, from India to Japan, possessed a splendid, almost cosmopolitan homogeneity, Central-Asian, Indian and Chinese influences mixing and alternating on the walls of a thousand shrines.

The possibilities of such a fusion are suggestive, more than ever so in the new awakened Japanese mind, impressionable, childish and eager for knowledge. The Japanese were discovering their innate gifts; and the frescoes, whether painted by Japanese artists working under foreign inspiration or by a foreign painter who had visited the Japanese court, mark a stage in the development of their national aptitude. Henceforward it was to flourish without hindrance—save for such hindrance as was provided by its own facility.

At that period almost anything might have happened. A trifle pathetic, knowing the future that awaited them, the readiness and eagerness of the Japanese, electrified by

their contact with the larger world that extended west-
wards to Gandhara and Sasanian Persia and, though but
shadowily, to Byzantium itself. China was their immediate
source of learning, and the great buildings of the Horyuji
monastery, the Kondo, the gate and the main shrine, are
designed with direct reference to Chinese models, wafted
in from Korea across the Straits.

An explanation of their quality would be very difficult,
since it depends not so much upon the form—that was
preserved by later Japanese architecture—as on the spirit
manifested in their smallest details, for instance in the
precise pitch of the curving roofs. Under these roofs a
heavy building appears light; the eaves, tilted upward at
the angles, seem to spread like strange wings as
one stands below, a convention, which was afterwards
to become static, having for the moment a look of bold
originality.

Even better is a small edifice not far away. This building, a few steps from the monastery gate, rises at the
centre of a cloistered courtyard. Legend says Prince Shotoku used to resort here; it was his oratory, a neat octagon
approached by steps and surmounted by a wide ingeni-
ously flattened roof that gives it a dignity out of all proportion to its size.

It is unassuming, simple yet somehow rich. Two cherry
trees were in flower as we entered the courtyard, carious
decrepit hulks, propped and bandaged, bent double, yet
throwing up into the air the gaiety of long branches
clothed with bloom. One might have taken them for an
image of Japanese art—that early art of which the gnarled
and twisted fragments still flower with such a freshness
even to-day, the tall statue against its duskily splendid

background, the pensive Kwannon whose raised finger touches her cheek.

And now the train was carrying us home across Japan. It follows—this line from Kyoto to Tokyo—the track of the old official highway down which the Shogun and his nobles used to pass, straggling between an avenue of tall pines, through the familiar Fifty-three Stages. A pedestrian monotonously broken landscape; low hills, dark and bristling as wild pigs, crowded together on the edge of the horizon, valleys neatly set with flooded fields where peasants wading and stooping in straw overcoats, men and women equally diligent side by side, resemble some odd breed of aquatic fowl. . . .

A village shrine, the beehive thatch of a farmer's house; it has changed very little since the Meiji, though the farmer now works by electric light. True, the high road is melancholy and vacant, and the steel thread, which has cut through and superseded it, presently runs into the modern city of Nagoya, a great blot of dim sordid wooden shacks grouped round the white keep of a mediæval fortress, slender chimneys pricking up against the sky and everywhere the awful squalor of the industrial world.

Nagoya, a city of millionaires; there is something peculiarly repulsive in Japanese industrialism, a huge expanse of smoke-stained wooden houses amid a labyrinth of narrow muddy lanes, all spawned by a gaunt factory or mill which towers above them with its pennon of drab smoke. Feudalism ground down the helpless peasants; it imposed on them that perpetual stooping attitude, up to the knees in the slimy sewage of their flooded rice fields; but the servi-

THE OCTAGON: HŌRYŪJI

tude of the modern industrial city is more degrading, more uncertain and as poorly paid.

Progress. . . . The train rumbles on, and, after Nagoya, one reaches districts that produce tea, small green bushes methodically dotted over the hillside. On and on; Fuji is out of sight, and towns become numerous and slipshod. They flick past in a grey glimpse of dishevelled roofs, interrupted here and there by a smoking chimney.

Factory chimneys, iron bridges, electric pylons; one cannot resist the thought when approaching Tokyo that these symbols of development and modern efficiency are erected with a certain histrionic lavishness. Never were streams so thoroughly bridged; every river appears to be spanned at several points by massive bridges, not all of them in use. Wires and cables looped eccentrically across the landscape suggest a large and clumsy entanglement for scaring birds. . . .

It was dark when we arrived at Yokohama, and only a thick sprinkling of fiery grains marked the suburbs which sprawl along the coast. Tokyo was preparing for the summer months, and presently the wet season of the year, with its sullen drenching days, warm and oppressive, began to beat into our tiny strip of garden. Or the sun came out brilliantly and the earth steamed. Red azaleas—our first impression of the house; we had caught sight of them from the road as we passed by, through the building which was a mere skeleton of sawn wood—brought back a time when it was new and when the green mats, creaking underfoot, and the thin framework of light beautifully fitting doors gave forth a delicious cleanly odour. Warmth and moisture had re-evoked that same fragrance; while black butterflies skimming through a shower and the rhythmic shuffle of clogs beyond the wall helped to waken a dormant sense of strangeness. Japan was as perplexing even to-day, as a year ago when we had moved in from the hotel.

A whole year was finished and put aside; it seemed to occupy very little room. Already it had acquired, if viewed in retrospect, the vague and dreamlike quality of our surroundings. It would be as simple to shake off as the house itself, which we should put behind us on the eve of our departure almost as casually as one strikes a tent. The delicate mats were rubbed and soiled by Western shoes; but no sooner had our luggage left the door than workmen would slip in by the back way and turn them like English tailors turning a coat. A few hours and their odd automatic industry would have removed the last traces of alien life.

INDEX

INDEX

W. R. GEDDES
Nine Dayak Nights

JOHN D. GIMLETTE
Malay Poisons and
Charm Cures

JOHN D. GIMLETTE AND
H. W. THOMSON
A Dictionary of Malayan
Medicine

A. G. GLENISTER
The Birds of the Malay
Peninsula, Singapore
and Penang

C. W. HARRISON
Illustrated Guide to the
Federated Malay States
(1923)

TOM HARRISSON
World Within: A Borneo
Story

DENNIS HOLMAN
Noone of the Ulu

CHARLES HOSE
The Field-Book of a
Jungle-Wallah

SYBIL KATHIGASU
No Dram of Mercy

MALCOLM MacDONALD
Borneo People

W. SOMERSET MAUGHAM
Ah King and Other
Stories*

W. SOMERSET MAUGHAM
The Casuarina Tree*

MARY McMINNIES
The Flying Fox*

ROBERT PAYNE
The White Rajahs of
Sarawak

OWEN RUTTER
The Pirate Wind

ROBERT W. C. SHELFORD
A Naturalist in Borneo

J. T. THOMSON
Glimpses into Life in
Malayan Lands

RICHARD WINSTEDT
The Malay Magician

PHILIPPINES

AUSTIN COATES
Rizal

SINGAPORE

PATRICK ANDERSON
Snake Wine: A Singapore
Episode

ROLAND BRADDELL
The Lights of Singapore

R. W. E. HARPER AND
HARRY MILLER
Singapore Mutiny

JANET LIM
Sold for Silver

G. M. REITH
Handbook to Singapore
(1907)

J. D. VAUGHAN
The Manners and Customs
of the Chinese of the
Straits Settlements

C. E. WURTZBURG
Raffles of the Eastern Isles

THAILAND

CARL BOCK
Temples and Elephants

REGINALD CAMPBELL
Teak-Wallah

MALCOLM SMITH
A Physician at the Court
of Siam

ERNEST YOUNG
The Kingdom of the
Yellow Robe

Titles marked with an asterisk have restricted rights